PLAY GIN TO WIN

play GIN to WIN

by Irwin Steig

GALAHAD BOOKS · NEW YORK CITY   776789

Published by Galahad Books, a division of A & W Promotional Book Corporation, 95 Madison Avenue, New York, N.Y. 10016, by arrangement with Cornerstone Library

Library of Congress Catalog Card No.: 73-82289
ISBN: 0-88365-079-7

Manufactured in the United States of America.

To Charlie—

Who so heroically fights the dawn.

CONTENTS

Chapter

1   **WHY DO WE PLAY GIN?**
Some of the reasons for the upsurge of this game   11

2   **GIN'S FAMILY TREE**
It germinated in Spain, and flourishes in America   15

3   **WHICH RULES?**
An exposition of Gin   18

4   **IRREGULARITIES**
You should know your rights   35

5   **GIN GALLERY**
Fourteen prototypes   41

6   **CHOICES AND CHANCES**
The essential mathematics   56

7   **ELEMENTS OF STRATEGY**
Foundation for a winning game   64

8   **DOES IT PAY TO SPECULATE?**
Pros and cons, mostly cons   77

9   **STARTING PLAY**
Early strategy and tactics   82

10   **DISCARDS**
Making and reading them   91

11   **THE LATE ROUNDS**
Any round after the fifth is late   98

12   **TEAM PLAY**
Two against two, or more against more   103

13   **THE CHEATS MOVE IN**
What you should know about their methods   109

14   **HOW TO REMEMBER THE CARDS**
Methods of strengthening recall   117

15   **WHAT'S MOST NECESSARY?**
Prime qualifications for a winner   126

16   **INVITATION FROM BIRDIE**
A night of adventure   130

    GLOSSARY
Gin terms in general use   138

    ABOUT THE AUTHOR   144

PLAY GIN TO WIN

Why do we play gin?

If a scientific survey of the card playing preferences of Americans were conducted today, Gin would probably take first place. Certainly more of us are familiar with the Rummy family of games than with any other, and Gin has become the most popular member of that family. Among men and women who would elect some other game, Gin is often the second choice; in a track meet method of scoring (so many points for first, so many for second) Gin would outdistance all the rest by a wide margin.

You have only to pass a modicum of time in places where cards are played to see that this is so. The Poker buff may have no patience with Pinochle, and the Pinochle buff may refuse to expose his wallet to Poker, but they are likely to find Gin common ground. Bridge players waiting for a fourth often turn to Gin, pleasantly to while away the time.

There are, of course, millions who find Gin so fascinating that they play any other table game only as a last resort; their number has been increasing continually and rapidly. What are the reasons for the upsurge of Gin? Why has it caught on in all strata of society, in all sections of our country?

"Gin is primarily a game for two, and that makes it convenient," says an engineer. "But it's adjustable. If three or more show up, we can all play."

"After an exacting day in court, when I'm tied up in knots," says an attorney, "Gin helps me unwind. It takes figuring, but it's just light enough to provide an enjoyable change of pace."

"It eases tension between rounds of a tournament," says a golf pro.

"There's plenty of big money action in Gin," says a manufacturer.

"I can get kicks out of it for small stakes," says his secretary.

"I found it easy to learn," says a beautician. "I like a fast game, and Gin is it."

"I took up Gin in self defense," says a housewife. "My husband used to get cranky when he couldn't arrange a game with his cronies. I let him teach me. At first he used to beat me; now I can beat him, and it's satisfying."

All these reasons for playing Gin are typical and valid. Add another: the intangible called taste.

Gin is not so vast as Bridge, not so intricate as Pinochle, not so violent as Poker. In comparison with those games, Gin is simple — it requires no elaborate system, no statistical study. But its simplicity is deceptive. Within its restricted area, there is room for maneuver and counter maneuver, for subtlety, for daring. A fight is not necessarily made softer by staging it in a small ring; the opposite may be true.

The player who approaches Gin with the notion that it requires neither science nor art inevitably departs suffering from abrasion of the bankroll, and laceration of the ego. I saw it happen last night.

Bob, an "occasional" Gin player, sat down smugly with Fred, an expert.

"You're going up against a Titan," a kibitzer warned Bob.

"Tighten, loosen, Gin is for children," Bob said.

"Who wants to grow up?" Fred asked in a tone you could squoosh on a sundae. "Hollywood?"

"Hollywood, San Francisco, you name it." Bob cut a Jack.

"The usual." Fred cut a Trey. "You deal."

Bob dealt; the upcard was the ♠10. They played

quickly, Bob a little more quickly than Fred, because **Fred** was thinking, whereas Bob seemed to consider thought unethical. The discard pile was still thin when Fred dropped a Queen on it. Bob picked up the Queen, discarded a 6, said, "I'll speculate."

"I won't." Fred pounced on the 6, and knocked with eight points.

"Nuts." Bob spread his hand. "Miserable lot of strangers." He found places to lay off a few. "Fifty-two. It could have been worse."

"It is. Spades double," Fred reminded him.

Bob sagged as he made a mental tally. "A hundred and four, another hundred for the game, plus twenty-five for the box. That's two hundred and twenty-nine."

"On the schneider," Fred said. "Four hundred and fifty-eight."

Bob was impatient. "Write it, and deal the next hand. I've got a long way to go to pull even."

Instead of pulling even, he kept falling farther behind. In deal after deal, Fred trapped him, trussed him up, speared him. At quitting time, Bob scribbled a check, and bleated, "I'd like to borrow your horseshoe."

It had happened before, and it is going to happen again. Bob, like other of his ilk, wards off the fact that Gin calls for certain techniques. "I never catch the right cards," he grumbles. Actually he catches his fair share of the right cards, but consistently does the wrong things with them.

Players who want to learn how to do the right things at Gin usually have to hunt hard for its literature. Few books devoted entirely to Gin are in print, and few copies of those are on sale. I arranged for a canvass of good stores in the county where I live, and this was the result: fourteen of fifteen stocked no such book; the remaining store stocked one.

The result was only a little better in big cities beyond the boundaries of this county.

I consider this state of affairs an injustice and an insult

to the people who play Gin, and who want to learn more about it — who want a shortcut to mastery of its strategy and tactics.

Surely you are entitled to the opportunity to read about your game, and to get the advantage that comes from doing so. My publisher proposes to make it convenient for you.

CHAPTER 2

Gin's family tree

Games of combination or structure, that is, games in which the object is to assemble certain sets of bones or tiles, go back to prehistoric times. Soon after cards were invented, people began to use them for such games. Gin is a modern development, and parts of its family tree are clearly discernible; the rest is conjecture.

Three hundred years ago, in many European countries, card games of combination were already well established. The Spaniards dreamed up one which they called **Con quien**, meaning, "With whom?" The object was to assemble three cards of the same rank, four cards of the same rank, or three or more cards of the same suit. Obviously, **Con quien** was a form of what we now call Rummy. The reason for applying "With whom?" to it is not clear. Idiomatically it may have meant, "Which card with which?" Or it may have been some sort of pun.

From Spain Con quien eventually travelled to Mexico, and thence to Texas and our other southern states. Somewhere along the route, the name of the game was changed to Conquian, which Americans pronounced Coon-can — Coon-king in some localities. Today, in English-speaking countries where it is played, it is usually Coon-can.

Because Coon-can and Rummy resemble the form of **Mah Jongg** originally imported from China, one might suppose that Mah Jongg inspired the inventor of Coon-can. But Mah Jongg is not old as such games go; it was unknown before the nineteenth century. So the more logical supposition is that the Chinese got the idea from Coon-can.

Some historians have suggested that Coon-can and Mah Jongg alike stem from Dominoes, invented long before the Christian era. Be that as it may, this is certain: in the United States, about the time of the Civil War, a new game was developed from Coon-can.

Because Poker is also a game of combination, Coon-can's new twig was first called Rum Poker. Rum is an old English word for queer, and may have seemed appropriate to the Poker players in the frontier saloons. Or perhaps they wanted to distinguish it from Whiskey Poker, while retaining liquor terminology. I suggest that it happened this way:

Somebody was asking, "What'll we call this queer kind of Poker?"

The bartender was asking, "What'll you have?"

A customer hollered, "Rum!" and that was it.

Over the years, Rum Poker was shortened to Rum, then lengthened to Rummy. It proved to be an exceedingly pliable game; hundreds of forms have been developed.

Gin, under some other name, was probably developed late in the nineteenth century; nobody knows exactly when, where, or by whom. Early in this century, it was described in print under the name Gin Poker. That forms of Rummy should have been identified with Poker so persistently is strange, because the games are so different in spirit and in technique. Rummy is a card management game; the skill consists in playing your cards so as to give you the best chance of getting the sets you need — and, of course, preventing your opponent from getting the sets he needs. Poker is a money management game; in most variations you have no control of the cards whatsoever, and the skill consists in playing out your money so as to get the greatest possible return.

By about 1910, Gin Poker had become Gin Rummy, or just Gin.

At first, Gin was quietly sequestered among the many forms of Rummy, and its devotees were relatively few. During the depression of the late twenties and early thirties, its popularity grew substantially; money was hard to come by, and Gin could be exciting at low stakes. In many homes it was played for mere token stakes, or no stakes at all.

When Gin became a Hollywood craze about twenty-five years ago, it was widely publicised. But Gin had been on the march in the East at least five years earlier. I remember visiting a Gin club in New York in 1933, and there were not enough tables for all who wanted to play. A rival club was also doing well. Nor was this trend confined to New York; I saw plenty of Gin action in other eastern cities, and in the Midwest.

Gaining impetus in the forties, Gin spread through all the states. Some of my California friends insist the Hollywood community did the most to make Gin colossal. They may be right.

CHAPTER 3

Which rules?

Before we dig into strategy and tactics, I think we had better determine *exactly* what game we are playing. The most extensively played variation of Gin has several sub-variations, and while they are similar —while you are sure to do well at any if you can consistently do well at one — a review of the rules should be helpful.

For the beginner, learning the rules is obviously a must; but I do not intend this chapter for him alone.

I take sharp issue with the type of instructor who says, "If you are an experienced player, skip the rules, and hurry along to the advanced stuff." These are my reasons:

1) What an experienced player may regard as generally accepted rules may be local practices, or mere "house rules."

2) Many experienced players are unaware of their rights when irregularities occur; knowledge of the rules can avert protracted debate.

3) Knowledge of the rules commands respect, providing a psychological advantage. I am not proposing that you emulate the pundit who cites chapter and verse whenever somebody is guilty of an inconsequential infraction; I am sure you can use the knowledge with discretion.

Let it be clearly understood that there are no "official" rules for Gin, because it is not an organized sport or business with a governing body. Nor is there a universally recognized individual to say, "Oh my beloved followers, this is the only way to play." If anybody tried to arrogate such powers to himself, the people in that delightful anarchy called Gin would thumb their noses at him — between deals.

But there has to be a basic code of practices, and there is — a code established by tradition. Many good-enough versions of this code have been published; no two agree about everything — no two of the various "Hoyles" are in complete accord about Gin. Nevertheless common sense prevails, and the game is about the same everywhere. Incidentally the original Hoyle, Edmond, never wrote a word about Gin; he lived two centuries ago.

The rules and procedures set down here apply in most places where I have played or observed Gin. To make this code national in scope, I have checked details with authentic experts in all sections of the United States. If you play Gin by this code, you can easily adjust to the practices of any group you may join. Right now some group may be agreeing gleefully to let the ♣8 snazzle the ♡5, and you may find yourself pitted against one of its members tomorrow. If that happens, let him explain the innovation; for all I know, it may improve the game.

The Cards. The standard fifty-two card deck is used. Make sure no card is missing — see the chapter on cheating. Even when you play with friends you trust without reservation. make sure of this; somebody may be careless.

The cards rank so in descending order:

K Q J 10 9 8 7 6 5 4 3 2 A. The K is always high; the A is always low.

Point values are assigned to the cards: ten points for any picture card — any K, Q or J. From the 10 down to the Deuce, each card has its pip value — 10 points for a 10, nine points for a 9, and so on. An A counts one point.

All the suits have the same rank in the play of the hand.

Who Deals? At the start of the first game, this is determined by cutting, informally in most circles. Elsewhere the complete deck is fanned out face down on the table, and none of the two cards at either end may be cut — a stuffy little provision. If opponents cut cards of the same rank, the suits are given rank to break the tie, as follows: in descending order, Spades, Hearts, Diamonds, Clubs — as at Bridge.

The player who cuts the high card decides who shall deal. Almost always he automatically decides that his opponent shall deal, because the non-dealer will play first, and there is some advantage in that. Therefore the player who cut the low card usually deals without palaver.

After a hand has been completed, the winner deals the next hand, as is sporting.

If a hand ends in a tie, the player who dealt it deals again.

Usually several hands must be played to complete a game. In any case, if the same opponents decide to play another game, the winner usually deals the first hand. In some circles, every new game begins with a new cut.

Shuffle and Cut. The non-dealer may shuffle the deck if he so chooses; the dealer has the right to shuffle last. The non-dealer then cuts the deck, and the deal proceeds.

The Deal. The dealer gives the first card to his opponent, the second card to himself, and continues alternating this way until each player has ten cards.

The rest of the deck constitutes the *stock*, which is placed face down on the table.

At this stage there are two different, established procedures:

1) This is the procedure in regular Gin Rummy. The dealing chore finished, the non-dealer picks up and adds to his hand the top card from the stock, preparatory to starting play. To save a moment, the dealer may give an eleventh card to the non-dealer — same thing.

The knocking count is ten. I shall explain about knocking, and about going Gin, in the proper places.

2) This alternative creates a variation which is called Oklahoma Gin in most circles — Long Island or Cedarhurst

Gin in some circles. Do not confuse it with just Oklahoma, which is another form of Rummy, and not closely related.

In Oklahoma Gin, after each player has ten cards, and the stock is down, the dealer turns up the top card from the stock. He puts this upcard beside the stock, starting the discard pile. Now the non-dealer has a choice: he may add to his hand the upcard, or the top card from the stock. If the non-dealer refuses to pick the upcard, the dealer may pick it.

If the upcard is a Spade, the score is doubled. This gives the player who is behind a chance to catch up or go ahead in a jiffy; it can also hasten his debacle.

Oklahoma Gin is the sharper, more difficult variation.

As if "Spades double" were not sharp enough, some players borrow a Backgammon gimmick: "Hearts quad." This means that if the upcard is a Heart the score is quadrupled.

To my mind, "Hearts quad" is contrary to the spirit of Gin, and most players seem to agree.

First Objective. Each player tries to accumulate combinations of cards called sets — also called lays, melds or runs. A set consists of three or four cards of the same rank; or three or more consecutive cards in the same suit. Examples of sets follow:

♠	♡	♢	♣	♢	♡	♠	♡	♡	♡	♠	♠	♠	♠
6	6	6	J	J	J	J	K	Q	J	9	8	7	6

♡	♡	♡
3	2	A

The following is not a set in regular Gin, or Oklahoma Gin, because the A is low only and may not be used above the K:

♠	♠	♠
A	K	Q

The following is not a set because, while the cards are in sequence, they are not in the same suit:

♡	♡	♢
8	7	6

The following is not a set because, while the cards are in the same suit, they are not in sequence:

♣ ♣ ♣
J 9 8

No one card may be used simultaneously in two sets. Consider the following example:

♠ ♡ ♣ ♣ ♣
7 7 7 6 5

Here you have three 7's, and the ♣7 6 5. You are not permitted to use the ♣7 simultaneously both ways; you must decide whether to consider the three 7's a set, or the three consecutive Clubs a set. Distinguish between the foregoing and the following:

♠ ♡ ◇ ♣ ♣ ♣
7 7 7 7 6 5

Here your ♠7 ♡7 ◇7 constitute one set; your ♣7 ♣6 ♣5 constitute a second set.

Sometimes you can combine the identical cards into different series of sets — according to rank, or according to suit and sequence. Consider the following example:

♠ ♡ ♣   ♠ ♡ ♣   ♠ ♡ ♣
5 5 5   4 4 4   3 3 3

♠ ♠ ♠   ♡ ♡ ♡   ♣ ♣ ♣
5 4 3   5 4 3   5 4 3

Unless you have been the victim of an optical illusion, you have readily seen that the cards are identical, but combined in different ways. Which way you combine the sets would matter only if your tenth card extended one of the sets. If your tenth card were another 5, 4 or 3, you would combine your sets according to rank, because the 5, 4 or 3 would then extend one of those sets. If your tenth card were the ♠6 or 2, the ♡6 or 2, or the ♣6 or 2, you would combine your sets according to suit and sequence, for the same reason.

The cards which do not fall into sets are called deadwood. Obviously, the more sets you hold, or the greater their length, the less your deadwood. As you accumulate sets, your first objective is, simultaneously and automatically, to reduce your deadwood.

Later Objectives. Once in a very long while you will be dealt a hand in which all ten cards fall into sets — a hand which enables you to go Gin. Here are a few such hands:

♠	♡	◇	♣		♡	◇	♣		♠	◇	♣
J	J	J	J		9	9	9		2	2	2

♠	♡	◇	♣		◇	◇	◇		♣	♣	♣
8	8	8	8		6	5	4		6	5	4

♠	♠	♠	♠		♡	♡	♡		◇	◇	◇
10	9	8	7		K	Q	J		3	2	A

♡	♡	♡	♡	♡	♡	♡	♡	♡	♡
10	9	8	7	6	5	4	3	2	A

All tidy, beautiful, and often elusive. Usually you will have to play precisely if you hope to go Gin, and a skilled opponent may make it difficult if not impossible. When you go Gin you always win the box — more about boxes under *scoring*.

Theoretically the ultimate objective in any deal is to go Gin, but there is an alternative objective — an objective which is often more practicable and profitable:

To knock.

When you reach the knocking count, you have the right to terminate the deal. By doing so you will not always win it; an element of risk is involved.

At regular Gin, the knocking count is always ten. To reach it, you must reduce the count of your deadwood to ten points or less. Here is an example:

♠	♡	◇	♠		◇	◇	◇		♠	♡	♣
J	J	J	J		8	7	6		4	4	2

The deadwood in your hand is the ♠4 ♡4 ♣2, adding up to ten points; you have the right to knock.

Consider this hand:

♠	♡	◇	♣		◇	◇	◇		♠	♡	♣
J	J	J	J		8	7	6		5	4	2

The deadwood in your hand adds up to eleven points. You must reduce that to win the right to knock.

Play. Holding eleven cards, the non-dealer starts by discarding one. The dealer picks the discard, *or* the top card from the stock; then he discards one card. The players alternate in this maner until either of them decides to knock or can go Gin. If, when the stock is down to only two cards, neither player has knocked or gone Gin, play stops and the deal is voided — it is a stand-off with no score for either player.

Where Gin is taken seriously, the discard pile is neatly maintained, with only the face of the top card visible — digging into the pile to examine previous discards is unthinkable. Elsewhere this efficient method of refreshing the recollection may be permitted. Opponents may achieve a cozy little compromise, spreading the discards about with studied carelessness so that the faces of most if not all stare up demurely. It is up to you and your opponent to decide what kind of game you want.

At Oklahoma Gin, the first upcard — the one which establishes the knocking count — is put aside, so that there may never be any doubt about it. If that card is picked up or buried, either player may at any time verify the knocking count.

Going Gin. When a player can go Gin, he turns his discard face down; then he lays his hand face up on the table, melding his sets. This whole procedure is called *going down*. He gets the Gin bonus, which is twenty-five points in most circles — only twenty in some circles — and whatever whim dictates elsewhere.

The other player then turns his hand face up on the table, and melds any sets he may have. His deadwood count is added to the winner's Gin bonus for one box. For example, Al chirps, "Whassa name of this game?" as he goes down with his hand:

♠	♡	◇	♣		♡	♡	♡		◇	◇	◇
2	2	2	2		10	9	8		7	6	5

"All I needed was one lousy card," Tom says, as he turns up this hand:

♠	♡	◇		♠	♠	♠		♣	♣	♣		♡
Q	Q	Q		9	8	7		8	7	6		J

Tom melds his sets. His deadwood is the ♡J, which counts ten. Al adds ten to his Gin bonus; he scores the total, thirty-five, for the box.

Tom consoles himself by saying, "I knew you were looking for the Jackahearts; that's why I held onto it."

Knocking and Laying Off. When a player knocks, he turns his discard face down; then he turns his hand face up on the table, melding his sets. His deadwood is his count.

The non-knocker then turns his hand face up on the table, melding his sets. There is a complication, laying off, which may reduce his deadwood. For example, Tom knocks with this hand:

♡	◇	♣		◇	◇	◇	◇		♠	♡	◇
6	6	6		Q	J	10	9		4	A	A

The deadwood in Tom's hand adds up to a count of six. Al turns up this hand:

♠	♡	◇	♣		♠	◇	◇	♣	♣
3	3	3	3		6	8	7	8	7

That is a sorry lot of deadwood — but wait! Al has the right, wherever possible, to lay off his deadwood. This means he may use his deadwood to extend Tom's sets. Accordingly, Al lays off his ♠6 against Tom's three 6's; Al lays off his ◊8 7 against Tom's ◊Q J 10 9. Al's deadwood is now reduced to the ♣8 7, which count 15.

Tom subtracts his six points from Al's fifteen. Tom scores the difference, nine, for the box.

As previously pointed out, there is a risk in knocking, especially at a late stage of the deal: the knocker may be *undercut*, suffering a stiff penalty. An undercut occurs when the non-knocker's deadwood equals **or** falls below the knocker's. For example, Al knocks optimistically with this hand:

♠	♡	♣		◊	◊	◊	◊		♠	♡	♣
5	5	5		10	9	8	7		6	2	A

Al's deadwood count is nine, but Tom turns up this hand:

♠	♡	◊	♣		◊	◊	◊	◊	◊	♣
K	K	K	K		J	6	5	2	A	A

Tom melds his four K's. He lays off his ◊J and ◊6 5 at the ends of Al's ◊J10 9 8 7. After the laying off, the hands look so:

Al —
♠	♡	♣		◊	◊	◊	◊	◊	◊	◊		♠	♡	♣
5	5	5		J	10	9	8	7	6	5		6	2	A

Tom —
♠	♡	◊	♣		◊	◊	♣
K	K	K	K		2	A	A

Al's deadwood still totals nine points, but Tom's deadwood now totals only four. The difference is five, in Tom's favor. Tom adds the five to the undercut penalty which is twenty-five. Tom's score is thirty points.

In some circles the undercut penalty is only twenty; that unbalances the game unless the Gin bonus is made the same as the undercut penalty.

Scoring. Having learned the objectives and the mechanics of play, the beginner tends to become impatient when the scoring is explained. He is likely to say, "Deal, somebody. I'll catch on to the scoring as we go along."

Such an approach is not entirely unreasonable; it can work out well enough where the beginner promptly applies himself to the chore of learning the minutiae of scoring. Unfortunately for him, he does not do so in every case; he may bumble along for months or years, oblivious to the hazards involved in the way points are credited, and at the mercy of the sloppy score-keeper or the sharpshooter.

What would you think of a quarterback who did not know exactly the respective values of a touchdown, conversion, field goal, and safety. Absurd? It is equally absurd at Gin to be unfamiliar with the various bonuses.

Getting a clear understanding of the scoring at Gin before starting to play is the orderly way. It will not take you long.

First, the winner of each deal gets a score of one point or more; the loser gets zero. Recapitulating, if the winner has gone Gin, he gets the Gin bonus plus the count of the loser's deadwood. If the winner has knocked, he gets the difference between his and the loser's net deadwood counts. If the winner is the undercutter, he gets the difference between his and the knocker's net deadwood counts, plus the undercut bonus.

In addition, the winner of each deal is credited with a *box*, also called line, but this is not tallied until the end of the game. The bonus for each box is twenty-five.

Whoever first reaches or goes over one hundred points wins the game. At Oklahoma Gin, with its "Spades double" proviso, the game is sometimes extended to one hundred and fifty points.

Either way, the winner of a game gets a game bonus of one hundred points.

When a deal is played at "Spades double," the score which immediately results from it is doubled; the box score is not affected. In some circles, all scores which result from a

"Spades double" deal are doubled. Always be sure you and your opponent understand, before the first deal, exactly what "Spades double" means in your game.

If the loser of a game has failed to get a box, that is, if he has lost every deal, it is called a *shut-out* — also schneider, schneid, blitz, or skunk, according to taste in terminology. In a shut-out, all scores which accrue to the winner are doubled.

Now let us score a game between Al and Tom.

In the first game, Al goes Gin, catching Tom with a deadwood count of eleven. That, added to the Gin bonus, makes a total of thirty-six points for Al, written as follows:

Al	Tom
36	

In the second deal, Tom knocks, and the rectified deadwood difference is fourteen in Tom's favor, written as follows:

Al	Tom
36	14

In the third deal, Tom knocks, but Al undercuts him by one. Al gets one plus the undercut bonus of twenty-five. *Usual practice is to keep a progressive score;* the twenty-six points Al has just won are added to his previous score, as follows:

Al	Tom
36	14
62	

In the fourth deal, it is "Spades double." Al goes Gin, catching Tom with a deadwood count of ten. Added to the Gin bonus, it comes to thirty-five, which is doubled, and the score is written as follows:

Al	Tom
36	14
62	
132	

As you have seen, Al's score has gone over one hundred; he has won the game. Now the score is adjusted.

Each box is worth twenty-five points. Al has won three boxes for a total of seventy-five. Tom has won one box. Therefore twenty-five points are deducted from Al's seventy-five, giving him a net box bonus of fifty.

A glance at the score will show you that Al has won two boxes more than Tom; usual practice would be to save a step, automatically crediting Al with fifty points.

For having won the game, Al gets an added bonus of one hundred points.

Finally Tom's fourteen points are deducted from Al's total. The complete final score follows:

Al	Tom
36	14
62	
132	
+50	
182	
+100	
282	
–14	
268	

They play another game. In the first deal, with "Spades double," Tom goes Gin, catching Al with a deadwood count of twenty-six. Added to the Gin Bonus, that comes to fifty-one, which is doubled. Tom has won the game in one deal; Al has been shut out. Tom gets a box bonus of twenty-five, plus the game bonus of one hundred, and this total is doubled. The score is written as follows:

Al	Tom
	102
	+25
	127
	+100
	227
	x2
	454

A shut-out on top of a "Spades double" deal can be a thing of beauty for the winner — and a nightmare for the loser.

Hollywood is an excitingly wacky method of playing three games concurrently; it is *not* a variation of regular Gin or Oklahoma Gin. Hollywood scoring can be applied to either.

Suppose Al and Tom agree to "play Hollywood," meaning *score* Hollywood. They rule six columns on the pad; they head the columns alternately Al, Tom; Al, Tom; Al, Tom. The first two columns are for the first game, the second two columns for the second game, the third two columns for the third game. In general, this is how Hollywood scoring is done:

A player puts his first score only in his first column. He puts his second score in his first and second columns. He puts his third and all subsequent scores in his columns in games which are still in progress. He may have won the first game in two deals; in that event he puts his third score in his second and third columns. A score is never retroactive.

Al wins the first deal, worth twenty-one points. Al wins the second deal, worth twelve points. The two deals are scored as follows:

Al	Tom	Al	Tom	Al	Tom
21		12			
33					

Tom wins the next deal, worth eight points; it is his first score. He puts it in his first column, as follows:

Al	Tom	Al	Tom	Al	Tom
21	8	12			
33					

Tom wins the next deal, worth twenty-four points. It is his second box, so he scores it in both the first and second games, as follows:

Al	Tom	Al	Tom	Al	Tom
21	8	12	24		
33	32				

Al wins the next deal at "Spades double;" it is worth sixty-eight points. Since Al has already won two boxes — since this is his third box — he now scores in all three games. As you will see, Al' total in the first game has gone over one hundred; the first game has been completed. Al takes the bonuses to which he is entitled, and deducts Tom's points, as follows:

Al	Tom	Al	Tom	Al	Tom
21	8	12	24	68	
33	32	80			
101					
+25					
126					
+100					
226					
–32					
194					

Al and Tom go on with the second and third games; nothing that occurs in them will be retroactive. Tom is well along on the road to catastrophe; he is far behind in the second game, and in danger of being shut out in the third. Suddenly Tom "gets hot;" he wins four consecutive deals, worth respectively nineteen, sixteen, thirty-three and eleven points. Tom has won the second game, and pulled ahead in the third. The over-all score is now as follows:

Al	Tom	Al	Tom	Al	Tom
21	8	12	24	68	19
33	32	80	43		35
101			59		68
———			92		79
+25			103		
———			———		
126			+75		
+100			———		
———			178		
226			+100		
−32			———		
194			278		
			−80		
			———		
			198		

Al and Tom now complete the third game.

Many players maintain a Hollywood series at no less than three games. When the first game has been completed, they rule two more columns for a fourth game — the second, third and fourth games become the current series, and so on.

For some players, three concurrent games are not enough; they maintain a super-Hollywood series of four or five games. I know an accountant and an engineer who get together weekly for a five-star epic version — a continuous performance with as many games as possible always in progress. They keep score on large ledger sheets.

Gin for Three players. Each in turn may cut out while the other two complete a game. But all three may prefer to get into the action together, and this·can be arranged as follows:

1) One plays against two in a standard two-handed game. Suppose Al and Tom have just been joined by Vic. They cut.

Vic cuts the highest card; he plays against the other two — Al and Tom are partners *for this entire game.* Al has cut the "second-highest" card; he is the captain of the partnership *for the first deal,* meaning that he plays the hand, while Tom kibitzes, sitting close to Al. Tom need not be a silent kibitzer; the partners have the right to consult, but whenever they disagree the captain's decision is binding on them. This right is not necessarily to their advantage; they may confuse each other, and acrimony may develop. Moreover an astute opponent will draw inference from the manner of their consultation, even though they do it in sign language, or with grunts which are unintelligible to him. In some situations, he may derive valuable information from their finding consultation necessary to all.

A two-column score is kept; the partners use the same column. Each partner collects or pays out the full amount of the score. In other words, the solo player collects or pays out double.

After each game, the solo player takes a partner for the next. Usually there is a round robin; each player takes each of the others as a partner in one game.

2) This is really a different form of Rummy, but since it is generally classified as a Gin variation I include it.

A three-column score is kept, and each player is entirely on his own in what often degenerates into a brass knuckles type of contest. The players cut; low cut deals; "next-lowest" sits to his left. Dealing and play proceed clockwise. When there is a knock, the knocker's opponents lay off on the knocker's or one another's melds. A knocker with the lowest net count scores the difference between his and each opponent's count. If both opponents undercut the knocker, only the undercutter with the lowest count gets a score, a Gin-goer gets only one Gin bonus. Game is usually extended to one hundred and fifty, or two hundred points.

When a player has gone game, he adjusts the box difference with each opponent, and gets a game bonus of one hundred points. He collects from each opponent. The player with the "second highest" score collects from the player with the lowest score. It can be Gin with an admixture of knockout drops. The admonition never to play cards with strangers is distinctly applicable to it.

Gin for Four players. They cut for partners. The two who cut the higher cards play against the others; each member of a team plays separately against an opponent. Two games are simultaneously in progress, but the results are entered on one one-column score. Game is one hundred and twenty-five points.

In each game, the player who cuts low deals. If a player in one game knocks or goes Gin, the others may stop to observe the result, and to let it govern their subsequent play.

If both partners have won they add their scores, entering the total in their column. If one partner has won and the other has lost, the lower score is subtracted from the higher; the difference is entered on the score.

Suppose Al and Tom are partners against Vic and Zeke. Al wins by eight points; Tom wins by ten. Al and Tom have won eighteen points.

In the next deal, Al wins by fourteen points, but Tom loses by seventeen. Vic and Zeke have won the difference, three points.

Stand-offs are not replayed. A standoff counts zero for both players.

After each game, the players change partners. As at Gin for three, there is usually a round-robin; each player takes each of the others as a partner in one game.

Gin for Six or More. The team idea can be extended: three against three, four against four, and so on. It complicates the accounting.

When three play against three, game is one hundred and fifty points. It goes up by twenty-five points for each additional pair of players.

CHAPTER 4

Irregularities

Ordinarily, innocent irregularities which damage nobody can be laughed off. In a congenial environment, even damaging infractions create few problems; sportsmanship indicates what is just. But at times, among the best of friends, recourse to "the book" becomes necessary. A normally fair-minded player may be rendered unreasonable by the heat of battle, or a stickler's interpretation of a rule may be contrary to its true intent, or you may have to contend with a member of that small minority made up of hustlers and cheats. So you should review the rules covering irregularities, and have them at hand for reference.

The Deck. Before the first deal starts, be sure the deck is perfect — especially if it has been used before. Short decks will be treated at length in the chapter on *cheating*.

Imperfections in a deck are seldom discovered while the cards are being dealt; but if it does happen, a new deal with a perfect deck is in order.

If the deck is found to be imperfect during play, the deal is voided, and a new deal with a perfect deck is in order. What to do about previous deals with the same deck? There is no completely satisfactory answer. The rule is that previous deals must stand as played, although that may not mitigate resentment or suspicion.

"I needed the sixaclubs to go Gin," Bob complains. "How was I gonna catch it when it was on the floor?"

"Why didn't you look for it on the floor?" Joe asks.

Bob would like to know who put it there, but that question is packed with dynamite which he decides not to detonate.

The Deal. A player who starts dealing out of turn risks forfeiting the advantage of being the non-dealer and playing first; therefore it is both ethical and legal that the irregularity be called to his attention as soon as it has been noticed.

If a deal out of turn is noticed before the first upcard has been dealt, or before the top card has been picked from the stock, that deal is voided.

After the first upcard has been dealt, or after the top card has been picked from the stock, the deal must stand.

A player who has looked at any of his cards forfeits his right to ask that the deal be in proper turn.

If a card is face-up in the deck, or if a card is dealt face-up, there must be a new deal by the same dealer.

The Hands. Be sure you hold the correct number of cards before play starts; otherwise you invite a penalty, and it may be severe.

If a hand contains one card too many, or one card too few, and the holder has not yet looked at any of his cards, friends playing an informal game may settle the matter without a new deal. Why waste time? Better to take a card at random from the hand and bury it in the stock, or take a card from the stock and add it to the hand. But either player has the right to demand a new deal before the first draw; that is the correct, formal procedure.

During play, if it is found that both hands are incorrect, a new deal is mandatory. If one hand is found to be incorrect, and the other is correct, the holder of the correct hand may (1) demand a new deal, or (2) insist that play go on. If he insists that play go on, the holder of the incorrect hand must discard without drawing, or draw without discarding, until his hand has been corrected. He is then forbidden to knock until his next playing turn.

If a player knocks or goes Gin with a hand which contains too many or too few cards, he is guilty of an illegal knock, and is penalized accordingly. See *Illegal Knock,* next page.

Illegal Draw. At Oklahoma Gin, if the non-dealer refuses the upcard, and draws before the dealer has been given the opportunity to pick the upcard, the draw must stand. The dealer may still pick the upcard. The non-dealer may not pick the dealer's discard.

At regular or Oklahoma Gin, if a player draws out of turn, he must put the drawn card face up on the table. The offended player may then pick this card, or the top card from the discard pile, or the top card from the stock. The offender may never pick the illegally-drawn card. As soon as the offended player has drawn from the stock, the illegally drawn card if still exposed must be buried in the discard pile.

If a player, drawing in turn, sees any cards other than the top card but can go Gin, he may do so, because no damage has been done. If the top card enables the offender to knock, he must refrain from doing so until his next turn. Meanwhile the offender must put on the table, face up, any cards to which he is not entitled. Now:

The offended player may pick any illegally drawn card, or the top card from the discard pile, or the top card from the stock. As long as any illegally drawn card remains face-up, either player in turn may pick it until he has drawn from the stock. After both players have drawn from the stock, any illegally drawn card which is still face up on the table must be buried in the discard pile.

When one player has drawn but has not yet discarded, a draw by the other player is legal — with a restriction. Such an impetuous draw must stand, even though the player has not seen its face; he may not instead pick the discard.

Exposed Cards. If a player exposes any of his cards, there is no penalty, because he has already been sufficiently penalized — by himself.

Any card found exposed in the stock, or elsewhere — on the table, buffet, bar, chandelier or floor — is buried in the stock which is shuffled and cut; then play is resumed.

Illegal Knock. This includes illegally going Gin. If the knocker's deadwood count exceeds the knocking count because he has inadvertently discarded the wrong card, he is permitted to correct his error — except in cutthroat games. If he lacks this excuse, the non-knocker has these options: (1) He may accept the knock as legal. (2) He may compel the knocker to leave his hand face-up on the table until the non-knocker has completed his next play. Thereafter the offender must knock as soon as he can legally do so.

If the knocker's deadwood count exceeds the knocking count, and the non-knocker has exposed any part of his hand but has not yet begun laying off, the non-knocker has these options: (1) He may require the knocker to continue play, leaving his hand face-up on the table. (2) He may require the knocker to pick up his hand, and continue play with this proviso: if the offended player knocks, the offender may not claim the undercut penalty.

If the knocker's hand contains too many or too few cards, the non-knocker has these options: (1) he may demand a new deal. (2) He may require the knocker to leave his hand face-up on the table, and to discard without drawing, or draw without discarding, until he has corrected the hand.

Non-Knocker's Incorrect Hand. If it contains too many cards, he is not permitted to correct it. If he loses the hand, that's that with all of his deadwood counting against him. If he ties, he may not claim the undercut bonus. If he can undercut, the deal is a stand-off.

If the non-knocker's hand contains too few cards, his deadwood count goes up ten points for each missing card.

Scoring Errors. Both players are responsible for the accuracy of the score. Each entry should be, and usually is, checked promptly to avert injury to either player. But errors are inevitable, and may lead to acrimony. For example:

Vic and Zeke have just finished a game; the score, entered by Zeke, shows that he has won it. They are playing the next hand, but Vic is not concentrating. He snaps his fingers, starts studying the score.

"What's bothering you?" Zeke asks.

"That last hand." Vic points to the last entry. "You knocked with nine, caught me with twenty-three. That gave you fourteen net. Right?"

"What about it?" Zeke asks.

"Up to then you had seventy-seven." Vic lets it sink in. "How much are seventy-seven plus fourteen?"

This time Zeke adds correctly. "Yeah, ninety-one. I'm sorry. I wasn't trying to pull anything."

"I'm not doubting your integrity," Vic says, "but your arithmetic stinks."

Zeke is too embarrassed to take offense. "What do you want to do? We could correct the score, and consider this hand part of the last game."

"I suppose we could." Vic ponders the proposal. "No, I've been playing this hand wide open. If I'd known I had to defend against game, I'd have played differently." He becomes peevish. "Why don't you learn how to add?"

Zeke decides he has taken enough. "I'll ask you the same question. After all, you're supposed to check the score with me."

How would you settle the matter? You might ask your Gin-playing friends, and see how many different answers you get.

Before I cite the rule which applies, here is a related scoring foul-up:

Vic and Zeke are playing what should be the last hand in a close, hard-fought game — or should it? The score shows

Vic with ninety-nine points, Zeke with ninety-seven. Vic wins the hand, worth eleven points, making his total one hundred and ten. Just as Zeke is about to tally the box and game bonuses, he remembers something. He pauses.

Vic is impatient. "Go ahead and score it."

"Hold on a minute," Zeke says. "Before the last hand, I had eighty-six. That hand netted me twenty-one, making my correct total one hundred and seven, not ninety seven. I win this game."

"What'll we do with the hand I just won?" Vic asks. "Pickle it?"

"We could score it as the first hand in the next game," Zeke says.

"That might be fair, then again it might not," Vic says. "I've been playing to the score. For all you know, I could have gone on and won a bundle."

"All right, I'll give it to you." Zeke writes *bundle* in Vic's column on the score sheet.

Vic leans over to read it. "Wise guy. From now on, I'll keep score."

"Enjoy yourself." Zeke pushes the pad over.

Perhaps that will take care of the future, but what about the present? A sound, concise rule covers *all* scoring errors:

When play of a hand has begun, no previous error may be corrected.

CHAPTER 5

Gin gallery

How does your opponent usually play Gin? What motivates him? Do any established traits, any habits, mold his style? How do they mold it? When you know, you can more accurately predict how he is likely to play during any session; you can then more readily determine what, if anything, he is trying to accomplish in any particular deal. The first step is to classify his style — to see where he sits in the gallery.

Although there are millions of players, the gallery is short, for there is only a small number of prototypes. Kibitz each one briefly, and you will see that his style faithfully represents that of some man or woman in your circle.

Each prototype is a montage. To point up behavior characteristics, I have included details of occupation and mode of living in some instances. If the violinist from the gallery becomes the dentist in your circle, that will not matter at the Gin table. The question is: How does he perform there? Analysis of his performance should help you play the player, and that is as important as playing the cards.

The gallery is open. Come in. Look around.

BRAGOFF

Concert violinist Bragoff enjoys Gin after arduous practice, and while on planes or trains. The critics have agreed that he is a virtuoso on the violin; Bragoff is sure he is also a virtuoso at Gin.

"My accompanist, Gropchik, thinks he knows how to play

this game." Bragoff pauses to chuckle, lets the chuckle expand into a guffaw. "Yesterday I schneidered him in a Hollywood, all three games. The final hand was a stirring crescendo, an early knock at 'Spades double.' Today Gropchik was somewhat luckier, but I still won more than five hundred points from him. I would never dream of accepting his money; we play on what you call the cough. Thank heavens he is a better pianist than Gin player.

"Another of my pigeons is my manager, Uhlmann. I have no complaint about his handling of my business affairs, nor for that matter about the way he plays cards. At Gin, he is the one who pays the fiddler." Bragoff pauses to allow time for savoring of the gag. "Yes, from Uhlmann I always collect. It is peanuts, but I collect as a matter of principle. He is stronger than Gropchik. Uhlmann's head is full of percentages, but they are worth nah-thing against my intuition. Of course, I can play scientifically when the situation demands it.

"Then there's my son Igor, a brilliant boy now in his senior year at Puddleston Academy, not a musician I'm sorry to say, his inclination is to mathematics, which does not help him when he plays Gin with his papa, as he loves to do."

Bragoff does win often at Gin, but not for the reasons to which he ascribes the phenomenon.

Gropchik is a better Gin player than Bragoff. Early in their association, Gropchik trounced Bragoff before a concert — Bragoff had been restless, had insisted on the game. The trouncing so disturbed him that he gave a poor performance that night. Gropchik, who idolizes him, will not let that happen again.

Uhlmann is a Gin expert. He is also a shrewd businessman who knows when it is politic to play a "customers' game."

Igor is different. Bragoff married his wife for her beauty, not her intellect. Their son has inherited her genes.

In all fields of endeavor, you will meet self-styled Gin experts. Some of them are really fine players; most of them are average. In any case they are not dangerous, because they warn you beforehand. The man to suspect is the one who says, "Gin? Oh, I just play *at* it." He may be a hustler.

LATCH

Ever since the depression, for over thirty years, Latch has loved and lived with one game, Gin. He met and latched onto it when his blouse business was barely breathing. Gin meant no more pinochle, no more shows, no more books — not that he had been a heavy reader, except for the trade papers. Many an afternoon when there was nothing doing in his factory, and just about every evening, he played Gin.

To get the benefit of cheaper labor, Latch moved his factory to Vista, a town one hour from New York. In making the decision to move, he was aware of the popularity of Gin in the new locale.

Prosperity and television came along; the television helped fill in the hours between business and Gin. With success came local prominence; he was asked to join a group working for a better Vista. He joined; he gave of himself and his money in the cause; he won back some of the money in the Gin sessions after the meetings.

Now in semi-retirement, Latch takes a long vacation every summer at a luxurious mountain hotel. "The high altitude is wonderful for the lungs," he says. "Wherever you look there's a gorgeous view — blue hills, pine trees, flowers, birds, butterflies, you name it." He gets the view mostly through a porch screen; he stays on the porch playing Gin.

One day he took a walk in the woods. He had not gone far, when he met a crony. They analyzed the healthful effects of walking. On that theme, they continued walking together — instinctively back to the hotel for more gin.

Latch overwinters at a Florida resort, where he achieves an approximation of his summer routine. Once he tried Gin on the beach. At first he and his opponent agreed that the breeze was a blessing. As it became frisky with the cards and score sheets, they changed their opinion. They tried holding things down with pebbles and shells; that was too much bother; they soon abandoned the beach.

Returning from Florida without a suntan might mean loss of status. Latch gets his suntan playing Gin under a sunlamp.

At Gin as at business, Latch is an accurate calculator. He plays with concentration. His technique is without benefit of theory; his practical experience sees him through most of the critical situations.

IVY

It was no fault of Ivy's that her marriage turned rancid, ending in divorce. She is companionable and comely with gray hair and young-looking skin. She is intelligent, but blocks against mathematics, and has only average talent for cards. Because her friends play Gin, she took it up. To make sure she would hold her own, she studied sedulously, reading and rereading every Gin text she could find. She used the empirical method, too, setting up hands, and investigating the results of various methods of play.

The women regularly invite Ivy to their afternoon Gin sessions, but seldom to their Saturday night parties because of the shortage of unattached men. That problem is being solved.

On learning that men who play Gin congregate at certain resorts, she stopped at one such resort, and managed to get into some games. The devotion of most of those men to Gin was so intense that they were conscious only of her being a player; the others were under the supervision of wives, or if unattached, unattractive to her.

She tried another resort, and appears to have been more successful. An urbane widower, a Gin buff with a normal sex drive, is courting her. She is falling in love with him, and is clinging to him. She is careful to let him win from her at Gin most of the time; she listens attentively when he explains fine points which she understands as well as he.

"You've got marvelous card sense, darling," he says.

Her "card sense" is the result of work. Thanks to it, her game is competent — competent but not inspired.

POTZER

On loan from the Poker gallery, our old friends Potzer is a bungler at Gin, too. Away from the card table, he is no fool; but the moment somebody shuffles a deck, all of Potzer's intelligence seems to shuffle away. He is a member of that large segment of humanity which is without aptitude for games; nevertheless he gets pleasure from them.

"It's a harmless form of masochism," a doctor explains, perhaps facetiously.

"It's the sociability," Potzer explains. For his opponents, the sociability means acquisition of easy cash.

Gin for four with Potzer in the group usually means two separate games, because he is an excessive liability as a partner. He accepts the fact with good humor; he prefers solo games; he avoids exposing himself to bawlings-out from irate partners.

If you play Gin against Potzer, he will fall for the most elementary stratagems. When he holds a card you need, and it is not part of a set, you can depend upon him to discard it. You say it's a shame to take his money? He can afford it — he plays comfortably within his income. Why should the Poker crowd get *all* that loot?

CLIPPER

Contrastingly, Clipper has always been adept at games.

In youth he got his higher education at billiard academies, where he was dazzled by the polish of a pro called Velvet. Velvet used to say, "You demonstrate intestinal fortitude," and, "You're under a false misapprehension," and, "Thank you very kindly." Clipper patterned his behavior after Velvet's, and larded his locution with these expressions, plus others which he lifted from people who talked good.

There was a brief interlude in a mercantile establishment, where Clipper would not adjust to the discipline. Back to the billiard academies he went, for a post-graduate course which made him a full-time hustler.

"I'm always a little sorry to see a good customer get cut up," a proprietor said, "but I respect the classy way Clipper does the job."

As pool petered out, Clipper mastered bridge — without portfolio. He shunned the publicized tournaments; the easy money was in anonymity at rubber bridge. Eventually he made his headquarters at a non-membership club, becoming in effect an employee. He drew no salary, but was charged no card fees. He came early and stayed late, filling in at tables which were short a hand. When the tables were full, he was permitted to cut in wherever he chose. His courtly manner as he jockied weak partners made him popular among them.

Clipper had occasionally dallied at Gin. As inflation arrived, the Gin games became more numerous; there was bigger, easier money in them, so Clipper made them his province.

Beef, another hustler, once had the effrontery to try his art on Clipper. After playing the first game with feigned ineptitude, Beef suggested higher stakes.

Clipper's smile was regal as he said, "Thank you very kindly. You demonstrate intestinal fortitude, but I have had sufficient."

Later, to an intimate, he said, "Imagine that jerk trying such a gaff on *me*, the dean of them all."

Clipper's Gin technique is flawless; he contrives sharp psychological coups; he knows when, as a sporting gesture, to waive a penalty. Do not confuse him with the cheats; his edge is sharp but clean.

Last year, a bridge champion reputed to be an all-round card wizard, visited the club, and challenged Clipper at Gin. Clipper accepted. A friend called Clipper aside and said, "With so many fish around, why do you want to beat your brains out against him."

"He's too egotistical," Clipper said.

They played till dawn in a small side room, with kibitzers barred. The bridge champion's money flowed like ketchup at a battle in a movie spectacular. Neither of them ever mentions the episode. The bridge champion is jealous of his fame; Clipper wants none.

BIRDIE

Although Birdie left Richmond to go into the antique business up north in Vista twenty years ago, she retains an accent which she often makes more Alabaman than Virginian. Her husband's flourishing medical practice makes it needless for her to extract income from her shop on Joshua Road, but she rejects all offers for it. "What would ah do with mah time?" she asks "Ah just adore buyin' an' sellin' lovely ol' thangs." She sells them profitably; she is an astute businesswoman.

Always well groomed, Birdie wears a padded uplift, and there is plenty to lift. At parties she augments this with a plunging neckline, and prefers Gin with the men to Canasta with the women.

Sitting down opposite a new male opponent, Birdie leans forward, contrives a virginal look, and says plaintively, "Ah heard yo awfully tough. What yo-all goin' to do to po li'l me?"

The opponent, who knows what he would like to do, and may even nurture the notion that he will get the chance, mumbles something about being just an ordinary player.

"Ah sho admire yo modesty," Birdie sighs.

Unless he has been forewarned, the opponent concludes that she is defenseless; he decides to be chivalrous in the play of the hand.

As soon as the cards have been dealt, Birdie goes to work in earnest. Her mind houses a built-in computer, accurately programmed for Gin. Woe unto the opponent unless he glues his gaze to the cards, and keeps his mind on them. Woe unto him also even then, for Birdie is expert and merciless.

"Lucky me," she says as she goes Gin. "Yo-all can play rings aroun' me, ah know yo can, but tonight's mah night. Any time ah need a p'ticular cyard, there it is right at mah fingertips. Ah cain't seem to do anything wrong."

In the next hand, the opponent does something expensively wrong: he knocks illegally. "Yo impulsive boy," Birdie archly chides. The opponent, now completely flustered, involuntarily starts to pick up his hand. Birdie stops him cold. "Ah'm afraid yo'll have to leave yo cyards on the table fo juss a li'l while. It's the rule, ah believe. Correct me if Hoyle says different."

"Perfectly correct." The opponent leaves his hand exposed.

"Ah have to proteck mahseff, otherwise ah'd lose mah eye teeth," Birdie warbles. She extracts the full penalty.

She is in no danger of losing them. Curiously, even men who know her are sometimes taken in by her protestations. "She's amazingly lucky," they say. "It costs, but she's loads of fun at the table."

The wives snort.

JIFFY

Right or wrong, Jiffy is a quick thinker. Whatever the activity, he is distressed by delay. Anybody who does business with him will tell you that if your proposition is fair Jiffy will promptly close the deal.

He took to Gin because he found it fast, and wherever he sits in he makes it faster. He hustles through every hand like a commuter trying to finish the last game before the train reaches its destination. His friends say he developed the habit riding the commuter trains; actually he had always played quickly — he simply found himself in his natural element there.

Even in complex situations, Jiffy's playing is staccato, and he makes each discard sound like the snapping of a switch. When he knocks, he does so literally, giving the table a rap with his knuckles.

Lack of patience is Jiffy's weakness at Gin. Haste makes blunders — for you, too, if you permit yourself to be caught up in his rhythm, or to be unsettled by it.

SLUDGE

Making any kind of decision is a trial for Sludge, and he makes Gin a trial for any opponent. In a routine situation, Sludge will mull and muddle. In a complex situation, he will pull a card from his hand, put it back, pull it again, hold it poised as if ready to discard it, put it back, go into a trance. When at long last he makes a play, it is likely to be inferior.

Although Sludge is prepared to push up the stakes to a level which would normally stimulate desire in Clipper, Clipper wants none of him. The reason is economic: Clipper can finish several games with somebody else in the time it would take to finish one with Sludge. Other habituees of the Club avoid Sludge because he frazzles their nerves. But there are nights when he is the only available opponent for somebody who must have action.

Patience is more necessary than skill when you contend with Sludge. He plays slowly because he cannot play any other way. Needling him will not speed his pace.

WANDER

"What's the knock?" Wander asks. It is an early stage of the first hand at Oklahoma Gin, but already he has forgotten. He has forgotten also his and his opponent's discards.

"Five," says his opponent, who happens to be Potzer. Graciously, Potzer flashes the ♡5; it was the upcard, and he picked it.

Wander promptly forgets it, puts a cigaret between his lips, lights it. Play continues; Potzer discards the ♠10. Wander gives it a glance — his thoughts take this detour:

Spade — handle broken on my old spade, need new one — lazy son supposed to dig up patch behind house so wife can put in perennial bed — wife's birthday next week — jeweler asking stiff price for ruby-studded charm she wants to hang on bracelet — if bracelet gets heavier it will weigh ton — wife getting heavier in spite of diet — *I'm* getting heavier, suits tight, can't afford looking poorly dressed at business — skip martini at lunch, skip desert — some build on that waitress — would she go out with me? — bad idea to fool around with local talent — gossipy town — wonder how much my switchboard operator knows — some build on operator — motel order must be filled — price list needs revising — close out that lot of seconds — Anitra's Dance looks good in the second at Roosevelt Raceway tomorrow — Estrada pitches for Orioles tomorrow — heavy day at office tomorrow, no late session tonight —

Wander discards the ◊8, which enables Potzer to go Gin. The discard was so bad that even Potzer is moved to criticism. He says gently, "Didn't you see me pick up the eightaclubs before?"

"I thought it was the 6."

A kibitzer points out the ♣6 in Wander's hand. Wander looks at the hand; his cigaret drops in his lap; he retrieves the cigaret before it can do any damage. He melds four 6's.

Lack of concentration is Wander's undoing, and he realizes it. "Thinking of other things while I'm playing Gin costs me a few points," he says.

He does not realize how many *thousands* of points it costs.

CHATTIE

Like most other women and many men, Chattie considers a card game an occasion for light conversation rather than a contest. She took to Gin because it resembles Mah Jongg which died a few years ago in her circle. She used to talk incessantly through the Mah Jongg afternoons, and is giving repeat performances through the Gin afternoons.

Chattie plays, too. When it is her turn to pick, she reaches to the stock as if it were a grab bag full of inconsequential articles; her tongue is turned to other topics.

Because she knows what is going on in town and does not lack wit, she is usually interesting — to those who share her atttitude toward the game. To the others she is a nuisance. The serious players automatically win from her, without joy; they contend that the amounts are insufficient compensation for the ordeal of listening to her.

Up to a point, my sympathies are with Chattie. The purpose of getting together for Gin is to have fun, and conversation is fine when an opponent is willing to listen. But when an opponent wants to play the game, I think Chattie should compromise by keeping quiet half of the time.

WEEPY

Ask Weepy how he is doing when business is booming, and he will tell you with a shrug that he is getting by. When business is slow, you won't have to ask him; he will come sighing to you for advice and consolation. He needs neither. His real estate agency has long provided him with more than a mere livelihood; he owns valuable property; he is secure against the depression which he considers inevitable.

A television baseball fan, he follows the action in both major leagues. He pulls sentimentally for the Mets, but bets on the Yankees. His concept of a great game is what the players call a laugher — a game in which the issue is never in doubt.

One night a week, Weepy plays Gin for moderate stakes with other members of the local real estate board. He groans his way through each session, continually complaining about the cards which come his way.

"What does a man have to do to match up anything around here?" Weepy plaintively asks.

"Wait, I'll get a sponge to soak up your tears," somebody says.

Weepy picks from the stock, registers frustration as he re-arranges his cards, registers trepidation as he discards.

His opponent falls into the trap. Thinking he will catch Weepy with a load of deadwood, he knocks with ten.

Weepy undercuts him with two.

"What were you crying about?" His opponent irritably enters the score. "You were nearly Gin."

"The last card improved my hand," Weepy innocently explains.

From another table, somebody sings out, "You oughta know Weepy by now. Never listen to him, never pay him any mind, just play your hand."

It is valid advice.

COWBOY

For Cowboy, Gin is an open range, and the most beautiful thing on it is a perfectly matched hand. "Feast your eyes on that long straight flush, and those four of a kind," he says as he goes down with such a hand. "How I wish I could catch such cards at Poker."

The other player breaks the point of the pencil as he enters the score. "What's wrong with them at this game?"

"Nothing, absolutely nothing." Cowboy happily shuffles the deck.

A motley accumulation of unmatched cards may indicate close defense, but Cowboy prefers to play them aggressively. When his hand is better, he scorns the early knock — he prefers to try for Gin. It would be inaccurate to say he throws caution to the winds; he has no caution to throw.

"Win big, or lose big, that's my policy," Cowboy says.

It is an exciting policy which pays off to his opponents more often than to him.

CAUTIOUS

Whatever the risk, Cautious believes in holding it to a minimum, and his Gin strategy is an enunciation of that principle. He is not stingy; when he hosts the game his buffet is more lavish than that set up by any other member of his circle. But he plays as if his last dollar were at stake.

With innate pessimism, Cautious invariably rids his hand of high cards early, unless they fit into complete sets. Holding an unpromising hand, he is willing to defend all the way, closely watching the discards and making pertinent deductions — including deductions from his deadwood count.

"How can anybody play that way?" Cowboy asks.

"How can any prudent person play any other way?" Cautious retorts.

Essentially, Cautious's game is sound. Its weakness is that any opponent soon learns exactly what to expect from him. Friends have pointed that out to him, and he has listened. Half-convinced, he has at times resolved to take slightly longer chances. He has never been able to keep such a resolution.

PROTEUS

In Grecian mythology, Proteus was a god who could quickly assume various forms; in the theater *protean* describes an actor who can play many different kinds of roles — lightning change artists were so billed in vaudeville. The name Proteus fits this character in our gallery. He is an attorney whose courtroom histrionics win verdicts; his Gin table histrionics win points.

Proteus can convincingly feign naivete when he is spinning a sticky web for an unwary opponent, elation when he is meeting unwelcome strangers in his hand, despair when he expects soon to go Gin. His tactics follow no particular script; he improvises as he goes along. He may play one hand after the manner of Cowboy, and another after the manner of Cautious — without their errors.

At irregular intervals, he varies the order in which he arranges his cards. He may put his high cards to the left side in one hand, and to the right side or toward the middle in the next. He may utilize the same sort of pattern in several consecutive hands. He may slip his picks into his hand at random, mentally shifting them into logical locations — a method which might cause an ordinary player to blunder. An opponent who tries to glean information from these manipulations is likely to go astray.

Playing against Proteus one night, Clipper thought he had detected a recurring pattern in Proteus's card arrangements. To lead Clipper on, Proteus played a few hands with his high cards in the middle. Suddenly Proteus switched. Clipper was fooled; he confidently discarded as Proteus wanted him to. Proteus pounced, and knocked.

Ruefully, the art connoisseur in Clipper spake out. "You're playing a smart game, counselor."

Proteus enjoys sending out a salesman — a discard calculated to lure a card he wants from an opponent's hand. An opponent's discard may be useless to Proteus; that may be the cue for him to contrive an expression of uncertainty, as if he were contemplating the advisability of picking it. He may accompany the procedure with a bit of patter such as, "To switch or not to switch, that is the question," or, "Why do you tempt me?"

Often tricky, Proteus is always within the bounds of ethics. He is a consistent winner who does not seek soft opposition. He wishes Clipper would tangle with him more often, although there is no profit in that.

Clipper considers it a privilege to talk with Proteus, but taking him on as a client is something else. "It's not that I'm short of intestinal fortitude," Clipper has confided to him, "but Gin is my livelihood, so where's the sense in butting my head against a Rock of Gibraltar like you?"

✳

Having completed our tour of the gallery, let us now utilize what we know about the characters in it. Imagine that you and I are playing a hand as partners. We discard the

♠8, which seems safe. Our opponent picks it. We remember that two 8's are in the discard pile, so he cannot be trying to match 8's. We remember also that the ♠7 is in the discard pile, so he cannot be building a sequence downward. A sequence upward? He discarded the ♠9 a while back, and watched as we picked it. Is there a gap in his memory, or is ours at fault? What is going on here?

He discards a 5, increasing his deadwood count by three points. Peculiar. Who faces us across the table? Let us assume it is each gallery character in turn, and fit our conclusion to the opposition.

Bragoff. A Beethoven concerto is running through his mind; music and gin are not mixing.

Latch. He is over-Ginned. He needs a rest.

Ivy. She's in love.

Potzer. He has done it again.

Clipper. He is trying to set us up for a game at higher stakes.

Birdie. It is not like her to err, and such trickery is not her style. Our memory may be at fault.

Jiffy. He has derailed himself.

Sludge. It has been so long between plays, that he has lost track of things.

Wander. He is deciding to pay the price for that charm for his wife's bracelet.

Chattie. She is talking, and not thinking about the game.

Weepy. Some of the needling has probably penetrated. We shall stand on our memory.

Cowboy. He is showing off, hoping incidentally to confuse us.

Cautious. Excessive caution does not necessarily improve the memory. The error is his.

Proteus. It is clearly a trick. Let us show him that he has underestimated us.

CHAPTER 6

Choices and chances

Early birds at the club are sitting in a group as they wait for action to begin. Clipper, who keeps useful data to himself, volunteers a fact which has no practicable value: "Even if you played Gin around the clock for the rest of your life, you would never hold the identical hand twice — I mean probability-wise."

"Aaaaaa, I always hold the same lousy cards," Potzer says.

Uhlmann, Bragoff's manager, does not have to be diplomatic here. "They're not the same cards. It's just that you play them the same way."

"Potzer has really been running in tough luck," Clipper says. It is the anodyne he dispenses for all losers.

Latch gets back to the original proposition. "Last night I held a hand which was the same as one I held a couple of weeks ago."

"Do you know what the odds against that are?" Clipper asks. "Are you *sure* the hands were *exactly* the same?"

Latch, an honorable man, hedges. "Well, they were nearly the same."

"I know a man who has two heads," Proteus says. It seems to be a non sequitor, but he commands respect.

"Really?" Latch says.

"Well, nearly," Proteus says.

The group is convulsed. The conversation becomes ribald with quips about near-virginity and near-pregnancy.

Let us leave the group, and examine Clipper's proposition.

It is correct. The number of different ten-cards hands which can be dealt from the standard fifty-two-card deck is:

15,820,024,220.

Since a player who has just picked is managing an eleven-card hand, the number of different hands available for management goes up to:

60,403,728,840.

There is no purpose in memorizing such numbers. If somebody in your circle should wonder out loud how many ten card hands are possible, you can satisfy his curiosity by saying, "About sixteen billion." That is close enough."

Birdie would react to such a tidbit of knowledge by leaning forward, simulating awe, and saying, "Hahcum yo-all nevuh tol' me about yo mathematical prowess? Ah bettuh watch out."

In any deal, the other player also gets ten cards; therefore combinations and permutations for either hand must be based on forty-two cards. Actually, each player can start with one hand out of a separate total of:

1,471,442,973.

After the cards have been dealt, the number of possible hand-against-hand combinations comes to:

2,165,144,422,791,078,729.

Up there among the quintillions the air becomes rarefied, so let us get back to earth. Hands which differ slightly in content may be identical for playing the game. Consider this one:

♠	♡	◇	◇	◇	◇	♡	♣	♣	♣
K	Q	9	8	7	6	4	4	3	A

The complete strangers are the ♠K and ♡Q. Replace the ♡Q with the ♣Q — substitute any other combination of K and Q in different suits — and you have a hand which is *practicably* the same. There are many such cases, and they effect a great reduction in the number of playing situations. Still, there is enormous variety. That poses two questions:

Will elaborate probability tables help you at Gin? No.

Can Gin be reduced to a brief, workable set of principles? Yes.

Most of these principles are based on simple arithmetic. The resulting numbers are conveniently small; remembering them is not nearly so important as assimilating the *ideas* they embody. At Gin you are repeatedly confronted with the necessity of making choices, and it is sound tactics to make the choices which give you the best chances. You must know *which* choices to make; it helps to know *why*, because you can then find your way in uncharted areas.

First, the average number of plays needed to finish a Gin hand is from eight to nine.

If your hand is a freak, your opponent probably also holds a freak.

If your original hand is very good, promising an early knock or Gin, your opponent probably also holds a good hand. People tend to dismiss this by saying, "Oh, cards just run that way," but there is an explanation. When you hold matching cards, the rest of the deck contains less cards which would be strangers in your opponent's hand; he stands a better chance of catching matched cards.

The odds against being dealt a set in the first ten cards are three to two. After the first pick, it is an even bet that a player holds at least one set.

When you make your first discard, the odds against your opponent's being able to use it in a set are approximately:

K or A — five to one
Q or 2 — four to one
Any other — seven to two.

He may, of course, pick an A or 2 to reduce his deadwood count.

The best type of hand for an early knock contains two matched sets, and four or less unmatched cards. For example:

J	J	J	7	6	5	4	5	3	2
♠	♡	♢	♡	♡	♡	♡	♢	♢	♢

The smallest number of matched cards with which you can knock is five, because you cannot stretch a deadwood count of ten into more than five cards. Here is an example of such a hand:

♠	♠	♠	♠	♠		♡	◇	♣	◇	♣
10	9	8	7	6		4	2	2	A	A

The type of hand with the greatest number of chances of going Gin contains three sequences of identical rank; such a hand is shown on page 22, any one of nine cards will extend a set.

The worst possible legal deadwood count opposite a knock is ninety-eight. For example:

♠	♡	◇	♣	♠	♡	◇	♣	♠	♡
K	K	Q	Q	J	J	10	10	9	9

I have never seen a player stuck with so much deadwood, nor have I seen a deadwood count of more than one hundred, but it is possible without "Spades double." Do you see how? The non-knocker might put down more than ten cards, and the rule permits no correction.

Every Gin player soon sees that the K's and A's cannot be used in as many sets as the Q's and 2's — that the Q's and 2's in turn cannot be used is an many sets as the rest of the cards. *But the rest of the cards also vary in set usefulness rank by rank.*

Starting at the top with the K's, each rank increases in set usefulness until you reach the 7's; then there is a decline, rank by rank, until you reach the A's. Let us examine this systematically.

You can use a K or A in any of *four* ways to build a three-card set. For example, you can use the ♠K so:

♠	♡	◇		♠	♡	♣		♠	◇	♣		♠	♠	♠
K	K	K		K	K	K		K	K	K		K	Q	J

You can use a Q or 2 in any of *five* ways to build a three-card set. For example, you can use the ♡Q so:

♡	◇	♠		♡	◇	♣		♡	♣	♠		♡	♡	♡		♡	♡
Q	Q	Q		Q	Q	Q		Q	Q	Q		K	Q	J		Q	J

You can use any card from a J to a 3 *six* ways to build a three-card set. For example, you can use the ◇J so:

◇	♣	♠		◇	♣	♡		◇	♠	♡		◇	◇	◇		◇	◇	◇		◇	◇	◇
J	J	J		J	J	J		J	J	J		K	Q	J		Q	J	10		J	10	9

When it comes to building four-card sets, the J's and 3's decline in set usefulness; they are better than the K's, A's, Q's and 2's, but not quite so good as the rest of the cards.

You can use a K or A only *two* ways to build a four-card set. For example, you can use the ♠K so:

♠	♡	◇	♣		♠	♠	♠	♠
K	K	K	K		K	Q	J	10

You can use a Q or 2 *three* ways to build a four-card set. For example, you can use the ♡Q so:

♡	◇	♣	♠		♡	♡	♡	♡		♡	♡	♡	♡
Q	Q	Q	Q		K	Q	J	10		Q	J	10	9

You can use a J or 3 *four* ways to build a four-card set. For example, you can use the ◇J so:

◇	♣	♠	♡		◇	◇	◇	◇		◇	◇	◇	◇		◇	◇	◇
J	J	J	J		K	Q	J	10		Q	J	10	9		J	10	9

You can use any card from a 10 to a 4 *five* ways to build a four-card set. For example, you can use the ♠10 so:

♠	♡	◇	♣		♠	♠	♠	♠		♠	♠	♠	♠		♠	♠	♠	♠		♠	♠	♠
10	10	10	10		K	Q	J	10		Q	J	10	9		J	10	9	8		10	9	8	7

The longer sets are, of course, all sequences. A chart of the five-card sequences possible in any suit follows. You will see that you can use a K or A in only *one* such sequence; a Q or 2 in *two* such sequences; a J or 3 in *three* such sequences; a 10 or 4 in *four* such sequences; and any card from a 9 to a 5 in *five* such sequences. Simply count up on the diagonals:

```
K Q J 10 9
Q J 10 9 8
J 10 9 8 7
10 9 8 7 6
9 8 7 6 5
8 7 6 5 4
7 6 5 4 3
6 5 4 3 2
5 4 3 2 A
```

A chart of the six-card sequences possible in each suit follows. You will see that you can use an 8 or 7 or 6 in *six* such sequences, and higher- or lower-ranking cards progressively less. You can use a 9 or 5 in *five* such sequences, a 9 or 4 in *four* such sequences, and so on.

```
K Q J 10 9 8
Q J 10 9 8 7
J 10 9 8 7 6
10 9 8 7 6 5
9 8 7 6 5 4
8 7 6 5 4 3
7 6 5 4 3 2
6 5 4 3 2 A
```

A chart of the seven-card sequences possible in each suit follows. You will see that it is impossible to build such a sequence without a 7 — that you can use a 7 in *seven* such sequences, and higher- or lower-ranking cards progressively less. You can use an 8 or 6 in six such sequences, and so on.

```
K Q J 10 9 8 7
Q J 10 9 8 7 6
J 10 9 8 7 6 5
10 9 8 7 6 5 4
9 8 7 6 5 4 3
8 7 6 5 4 3 2
7 6 5 4 3 2 A
```

Sequences of more than seven cards are rare, but in connection with the arithmetic of Gin, the following should be briefly noted:

You cannot build an eight-card sequence without an 8 or 7 or 6; you cannot build a nine-card sequence without a card from a 9 down to a 5; you cannot build a ten-card sequence without a card from a 10 down to a 4. The higher up or down you go from a 7, the less useful the card for building sequences, considering all of them.

There is something curiously attractive about long sequences, notably to men and women who have had Poker experience, and such sequences are also valuable at Gin — up to a point. The pursuit of a freakishly long sequence can be costly; on being caught, it can become a liability rather than an asset, and we shall reach that subject in a later chapter. I have charted the six- and seven-card sequences primarily to help demonstrate that the ranks vary in strategic value apart from deadwood reduction. The curve which follows shows at a glance how the ranks compare for usefulness in building sets.

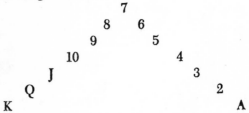

The recapitulation which follows takes deadwood reduction into consideration.

K — Least valuable, and the greatest hazard when not part of a set.

Q — More flexible than the K, but just as great a deadwood hazard.

J — More flexible than the K or Q, but just as great a deadwood hazard.

10 — More flexible than any of the picture cards, but just as great a deadwood hazard.

9 — Significantly more flexible than anything from a K down to a 10, but still a great deadwood hazard.

8 — Almost as flexible as the prime 7; as useful for building sets as the 6; but too high a deadwood count for comfort.

7 — Crapshooters, attention! The most useful rank in building sets.

6 — Only a shade less useful than the 7 for building sets, and one point lower in deadwood count.

5 — Flexible, and fairly good as a reducer.

4 — Flexible, and good as a reducer.

3 — Less flexible than the 4, but a better reducer.

2 — As poor as the Q for building sets, but valuable as a reducer.

A — As bad as the K for building sets, but the most valuable reducer.

In general — and remember that we are disregarding the effects of cards known to be in the discard pile — the most valuable cards in the deck are the 7's, 6's and A's.

CHAPTER 7

Elements of strategy

The teacher was instructing the class in the art of putting words in proper places to convey an idea without ambiguity. As a fillip to the lesson, she wrote on the blackboard:

you cannot   they move too fast   time flies

She told the puzzled class to leave each of the three groups of words intact, but to rearrange the groups so as to make one meaningful sentence. She provided this hint: "You'll need a semi-colon and a period." After some tinkering, the class got it:

You cannot time flies; they move too fast.

That was long ago. Since then, flies have been timed — and millions of Gin hands have been butchered through illogical or careless arrangement of the cards. Kibitz Wander on a night when his mind is skipping along somewhere beyond the periphery of the table. He holds this hand:

♣	♣	♡	♡	♢	♢	♡	♢	♣	♣
9	8	6	5	6	5	7	7	7	A

Wander sees three combinations to complete. He does not realize that he already holds three sets, and can knock with a count of one. All he need do is rearrange his hand so:

♣	♣	♣	♡	♡	♡	♢	♢	♢	♣
9	8	7	7	6	5	7	6	5	A

It happens often to Wander; it happens on occasion even to the strongest players. It may be due to a distraction or tiredness, and emphasizes the first element in any system of strategy:

Logical, careful arrangement of your hand.

In the foregoing example, the ♣A does not have to be placed at the right end; it can just as well go at the left end.

"Any child ought to know that," Latch says somewhat impatiently. He is right, but many adults who know it neglect at times to do it.

There is a small minority whose members can play out a Gin hand accurately without bothering to arrange the cards at all, inserting the picks at random. You may want to try it — perhaps you can do it without handicapping yourself. For most players, that method dissipates concentration on what has happened, what is happening, and what is likely to happen before the knock. The best advice is to start by arranging the original hand with an eye to chances for improvement. Suppose you have just made your first pick, and hold these eleven cards:

♠	♡	♣	♡	♠	◇	♡	♣	♠	◇	◇
2	K	3	7	A	Q	6	J	10	10	6

Any of several arrangements would clarify the situation for you, and here is an example:

♡	♡	◇		♠	◇		♡	◇	♣		♠	♠	♣
7	6	6		10	10		K	Q	J		2	A	3

The high card combinations have been put in the middle because most players habitually put them at one side; the example lays a little emphasis on the advisability of varying the locations of your high cards. If you habitually arrange your hands in the same pattern, an observant opponent will soon figure it out; then at some critical juncture he may learn something vital about your hand by noting the place from which you extract a discard.

In many of the hands illustrated in this book, sets and combinations are separated from one another. The purpose is obvious: to make the text more readable. But:

Don't create gaps between sets and combinations in your hand when you are actually playing. Horizontal and vertical separations are equally bad. For example:

♠ ♠ ♠   ◇ ◇ ♣
9 8 7   ♡ ◇ ♣   5 4 4   ♡
         K K K   A

You may find such separations expedient when you hold no sets or combinations; deception is another matter.

"Such admonitions shouldn't be necessary," Ivy protests. "Watching how an opponent arranges his cards isn't nice."

She expresses the attitude which prevails in many circles, and nobody can reasonably challenge it from the point of view of aesthetics. But if anybody should tell Proteus it is *unethical* to notice through his bifocals where an opponent is putting picks he wants to keep, and whence he is extracting discards, Proteus's answer would be, "Objection overruled."

I am not going to dilate on Gin ethics. The people who play this game know what is ethical and what isn't; each group sets its own standards. If a careless player keeps flashing his cards, a decent opponent will call attention to it. Staring across the table at the *backs* of an opponent's cards? It does not make the most beautiful of tableaux, but it permits counter measures. Proteus says, "If an opponent can gain an advantage by observing how I arrange my cards, he is welcome to it. All I ask is the same privilege." Most players will concur.

When play begins, focus on the first upcard and commit it to memory. This means both rank and suit. If the variation is Oklahoma Gin, where you have the right at any stage to check back, remember that card anyhow, because:

1) Your opponent may have forgotten it, and you do not

owe him the voluntary reminder.

2) Asking him about the knocking count may interfere with his concentration, and he may become rightfully resentful.

Remember every card you and your opponent discard. Remember which of your discards your opponent has refused, and which he has picked. When he refuses a discard, visualize the sets and combinations he cannot hold; when he picks a discard, visualize the set it may build. If you are not doing all of this now, I urge you to develop the habit. Observe and interpret, again and again, from beginning to end. Your interpretations may not always be accurate; even so they will be better than no interpretations at all.

Since the average Gin hand is completed in eight to nine plays, remembering and visualizing should not be difficult. When a hand takes longer, remember as much as you can, concentrating on what is most important. Practice will sharpen your memory, so that you will more often *know* exactly how to play, instead of being compelled to resort to a guess.

Every player who has learned how to score is aware of the high cost of the shut-out. It doubles the winner's final total, and can be murder at "Spades double." So make your first object in any game to:

Get on score. Do it as soon as possible. Even if the entry is only one point, it is your insurance against losing an extra hundred-plus points in the event that your opponent wins the game. If he is marching merrily along on the way to winning a shut-out, you should be willing to take risks to get on score.

Cautious, a stanch exponent of this principle, is playing against Latch. After five picks, Cautious knocks with this hand:

♡	◇	♣		♠	♠	♠		◇	◇	◇		♡
Q	Q	Q		9	8	7		6	5	4		9

Latch has a net deadwood count of eleven. Cautious enters the two points he has won.

Kibitzing Cowboy says, "For two measly points you go down with a beautiful hand like that?"

"You're overlooking that I'm off the schneider. What's more, the box is worth twenty-five points."

"But any one of six cards would have given you Gin," Cowboy argues.

"Zasso?" Cautious shuffles. "Two of them were dead."

Cowboy is stubborn. "I'd have taken the chance anyhow. I like to go whole hog."

"Yeah, whole hog and half-assed," Cautious says.

"What do you think I was doing in that hand?" Latch asks. "Kidding around? I wasn't far from Gin myself."

Knock early as a general rule, even where a shut-out is not involved. There are times when it pays to try for Gin. In fact, Gin may arrive early without coaxing; but usually it arrives late, when the other player has substantially reduced his deadwood count. Most of the big scores are won by knocking with counts close to the maximum, after only a few plays; that is when you may catch your opponent with an agglomeration of unmatched picture cards and 10's. Every additional pick would give him an opportunity to unload.

The unseen score is another factor. Suppose a knock would mean only a net win of four points for you, and you decide to wait. Your opponent picks, knocks, and wins two points. A swing of only six points? What about the box value? Instead of your winning a total of twenty-nine points, he wins a total of twenty-seven. The swing is fifty-six points in his favor.

When you go down, arrange your melds to your greatest advantage, and this usually means with the lowest possible deadwood count. For example, you meld:

♠	♠	♠	♠	♠		♦	♣	♠		♦	♦
J	10	9	8	7		2	2	2		4	3

Your deadwood count is seven, which you could have reduced to four by melding as follows:

♠	♠	♠	♠	♠		◇	◇	◇		♣	♠
J	10	9	8	7		4	3	2		2	2

If you know your opponent has an unmatched ◇6 5, or even only the ◇5 to lay off, the first arrangement, with the set of 2's is better — he cannot lay off against your deadwood. This is one of the many kinds of situation where a dependable memory helps you pile up points. Here it may mean the difference between winning the box and being undercut.

Be especially careful with your melds when you hold a four-card or longer sequence, in which an end card is also part of a set of four of the same rank. For example, don't meld these cards this way:

♠	♡	◇		♣	♣	♣	♣
9	9	9		9	8	7	6

If you make this mistake, your opponent may be able to lay off the ♣10 next to your ♣9 — he may be able to lay off the ♣J next to the ♣10. It may mean a reduction of as many as twenty points in his deadwood count. But he cannot lay off against a set of four of the same rank, so block him by melding as follows:

♣	♠	♡	◇		♣	♣	♣
9	9	9	9		8	7	6

Get the ♣9 away from the ♣ sequence so that there can be no argument.

Try to maintain a knock cache where feasible, that is, hold four or three or two unmatched cards which add up to a total of ten or less. It is better to match high cards than low ones. Suppose you deadwood is:

◇	♣		♠	♡
7	7		A	A

If you catch a 7, your deadwood count is reduced from sixteen to two. If you catch an A, your deadwood count is reduced from sixteen to fourteen. Sometimes you have no choice; often you can play with this fact in view.

Accumulate low card insurance where feasible against your opponent's winning the game. Suppose your opponent has eighty-seven on score — only thirteen away from one hundred — and you fear he will soon knock. You hold:

♣ ♣ ♣   ♡ ◇ ♣   ♠ ♠ ♡ ♡
K Q J   9 9 9   6 5 3 A

He discards the ◇2. Ordinarily, you would probably refuse it, preferring to try to catch a card which will extend one of your sets, or convert your ◇6 5 into a set. Any one of four cards would help you in that direction, but time is running out. If you can safely discard your ♠6, do so, and pick the ◇2. It will reduce your deadwood count to twelve, one below the total your opponent needs for game. He must go Gin to win it. You gain time, and that matters most now.

Do not interpret any of the foregoing as a permanent injunction against holding on to your high cards. There are many situations where you can profit by playing to match picture cards — many situations where you can take your opponent by surprise. Make it a policy to:

Vary your style of play from time to time. Be prepared always to take full and proper advantage of an opponent's inability or unwillingness to vary his style.

Speculation at Gin means picking an opponent's discard which will give you a combination — a discard which cannot immediately build or extend a set in your hand. Suppose you hold the ♠7 and ♡7, and your opponent discards the ♡6. Picking the ♡6 would be speculation. You would put it beside your ♡7, making this part of your hand look so:

♠ ♡ ♡
7 7 6

When you held the two 7's, only another 7 — one of two cards — could build the set. Now one of four cards can build a set: one of the two oustanding 7's, or the ♡8, or the ♡5. Taking only arithmetic into consideration, you have doubled your chances. Actually, unless your opponent is Potzer or Wander, you may not have increased your chances that much. Some of the cards you want may be dead. Moreover an astute opponent will try to block your completion of any of the sets involved.

Does it pay to speculate? Yes and no — more often no than yes. A brief definitive answer is impossible, because it depends on the situation, and so many different situations are possible, involving personality as well as arithmetic. Speculation merits a separate chapter — you will come to it. Meanwhile, a satisfactory generalization is:

Don't speculate with a good hand. Like most generalizations, it has exceptions.

With a poor hand, speculate a little. Never overdo it. If a bit of bold speculation brings about a minor miracle, do not repeatedly strive for major miracles.

When your hand contains five cards in which a sequence overlaps a set of three of the same rank, and you must break up one of the sets, you may find the choice difficult. Consider the following:

♦ ♦ ♦ ♣ ♠
6 5 4 4 4

If you hold the 4's, only the remaining 4 can extend the set to four — only one card can help you.

If you hold the ♦6 5 4, the ♦7 or ♦3 — two cards — can help you. You have doubled your chances. Moreover neither the ♦7 nor ♦3 will limit the sequence; you may be able to extend it still farther. For this reason:

It is usually better to hold a sequence of three cards than a set of three of the same rank.

In such a situation, the deadwood count may be a factor. Holding the ♦ sequence in the example just given, and dis-

carding a 4, would leave a 4 with your deadwood. Holding
the set of 4's, and discarding the ◇6, would leave a 5 with
the deadwood. It would work the other way if you held
these cards:

♠	♡	◇	◇	◇
6	6	6	5	4

In either case, there is a deadwood difference of only one
point, but it can decide the issue in a hand such as the
following:

♡	◇	♣	◇	◇	◇	♣	♠	♠	♡
J	J	J	7	6	5	5	5	2	A

You pick the ♡2. If you hold the three 5's, and discard the
◇7, your deadwood count will be eleven: too high for a
knock. If you hold the ◇7 6 5, and discard a 5, your deadwood count will be ten: perhaps low enough for a knock.

Extending a set at the expense of a live combination may
ruin a hand. Consider this example:

♠	♠	♠	♠	♡	◇	◇	◇	◇	♣
K	Q	J	10	7	7	6	3	2	2

You pick the ♠9, and your first instinct may be to add it
to your ♠ sequence. If you do that, what will you discard?
The ♡7? That will reduce your deadwood by seven, but will
effect another reduction: a reduction of fifty percent in your
chances of building a second set. Catching the ◇4 or ◇A
or another 2 will still leave you with a deadwood count of
thirteen. You may find yourself blocked, with nothing left
except picking and discarding as your opponent serenely
builds a Gin hand. The principle:

*Build a sequence of more than four cards only when it
helps the entire hand.* Consider extension of such a sequence
carefully with relation to your other cards. Sometimes, even
adding a fourth card to a set of three can be deleterious to
the entire hand, so be sure you survey the entire scene.

Switching to defense may suddenly become necessary. At the beginning of a hand, offense and defense are virtually indistiguishable, as you try simultaneously to unload your deadwood and build sets. You play primarily with a view to giving yourself the greatest number of chances; your immediate concern is your own hand. Later you may be compelled to play so as to limit your opponent's chances; blocking him may become urgent. For example, after about ten picks you hold:

♠	♡	◇		♠	♠	♠		♡	◇		◇	♣
K	K	K		Q	J	10		7	7		9	3

You know your opponent can use your 9 or 3. You pick the ♡8, and your first impulse it to put it beside your ♡7, discarding the 9. Not only will the 8 double your chances of building a third set, but also it will reduce your deadwood count by three. But you cannot afford to play that way. You discard the 8.

Here nothing can compensate for previous failure to observe and interpret. At Gin, as at the other major card games, there is a premium on close attention to detail.

The safest discards in the early stages of a hand are the A and K; next in safety are the Q and 2. A card of the same rank just discarded by your opponent may be a dangerous discard, for you must:

Beware of salesmen. At Gin a salesman is a card sent out by your opponent to induce you to err. Suppose Proteus holds:

♠	♡	♣	◇
8	8	7	7

Suppose he has reason to suspect that you hold the ♣8. He does not expect you voluntarily to part with it, so he decides to try some artful persuasion. He discards the ♠8 which becomes a salesman. If you discard the ♣8 because it seems safe, you have fallen into the trap.

If you play mechanically, you may discard the ♣8. Even though you play carefully, his salesman may successfully carry out his assignment. I hope you correctly identify him, and hold on to your ♣8. Proteus will probably unload the ♡8 next, and you can then safely unload the ♣8.

Never make a careless discard. If you hold intermediate and low combinations, and you pick one picture after another, frustration may make you impatient. But one of those picture cards may be exactly what your opponent needs to knock. And if it cannot help him, your discarding it with no more than a disgusted glance at it may provide him with clues to the general nature of your hand.

Every player makes an occasional manual error, usually when distracted or tired. Care holds such errors to a minimum. When you victimize yourself that way, as inevitably you will, cast it out of your mind as soon as possible. If you brood about it, you will make more errors.

You will not stall the game by taking at least one full second to study each pick, prior to discarding. If you do that, you will make the whole session last about three minutes longer. Surely you and your opponent can spare them.

Play the players. When you sit down opposite an opponent, ask yourself which prototype in the Gin gallery he most closely resembles. If you have previously played with him, check off in your mind his individual peculiarities.

Does he always unload high cards at the earliest opportunity?

How long does he hold on to high card combinations?

Does he habitually pick low discards which cannot help him build sets? Does he break up combinations to pick low discards even when his knock cache is adequate?

Does he speculate often? Occasionally? Never?

Does his general method of play remain uniform whether he is ahead or behind? If not, how does it vary when he is ahead? How does it vary when he is behind?

Does he betray impatience when he holds a poor hand.
How?

Does he betray impatience when he holds a good hand?
How?

Is he a resolution maker who soon goes back to his old
bad habits? Does his resolution last as long as an hour?

These are common peculiarities; there are many more.
Look for them, and exploit them. The better you know your
man, the better your game against him. Bear in mind that
a strong opponent is doing his best to know the real you.

Wherever Gin is played, you are likely to hear this open-
ing dialog:

"How about a few hands?"

"Sure, be my pigeon."

Often the alleged pigeon uses the other player as bird-
seed. While doing so he may indulge in some needling,
which is a legitimate part of the game. The ordinary kind
of needling is good natured and harmless, but there is another kind: strategic needling based on the sound principle
that an irritated opponent's game must suffer. You should
be prepared always to:

Blunt the needle. You may choose to deliver a witty retort
at some propitious moment, or to ignore the needling. Either
method will accomplish your purpose which is to retain your
poise, as long as you remain aware of what the needler is
trying to do.

Gloating can be a form of needling. When an opponent
goes Gin after one pick, catching you with a deadwood count
of about sixty, it is bound to shock you. If he behaves as if
it is the result of some unique talent he has, remember that
(1) he is showing poor taste, and (2) he must be insecure.
Else why would he gloat about a temporary triumph at
cards?

There was a night when a gloater playing against Proteus
sent out a salesman, and Proteus had no way of knowing it.

His discard completed a set for the gloater, who promptly knocked. With a smirk the gloater said, "You certainly distribute the manna."

Proteus said nothing. The gloater kept up a yak-yak-yak of cornball needling as Proteus won the next hand, and the next, and the next.

When the session was over, and the gloater paid, he said, "I couldn't get much of a rise out of you."

"But I certainly got a rise out of you," Proteus answered. "It's on my score."

CHAPTER 8

Does it pay to speculate?

Cowboy and Cautious are waiting for the club attendant to bring cards and a score pad. Potzer, hoping a suitable opponent will soon arrive, sits down to kibitz. A lull in the pregame conversation gives Potzer an opportunity to raise an issue which has been perplexing him: "When should a man speculate in this game?"

The answers come like successive machine gun shots.

From Cowboy: "Whenever you think you can get away with it."

From Cautious: "Never."

The attendant is on the telephone, so Clipper fetches the cards and pad. Potzer decides to put the issue up to Clipper: "I just asked these gentlemen a technical question about Gin, and got two different answers."

"Naturally," Clipper says.

"I'd like to get your opinion, professor." Potzer rephrases the question. "Does it pay to speculate at Gin?"

"It's an academic question." Clipper decides on an equivocal answer. "Speculation has its good points and its fallacies."

Potzer smothers a giggle. "Okay, but more of which?"

"Every player has to find a happy medium for himself." It is Clipper's final dictum, and he walks away. He does not want to prolong the discussion for fear of disturbing the players. He feels somewhat guilty, for he knows that in the area of speculation there is no happy medium; there is only an uncertain off-center point far toward the negative.

Speculation at Gin is roughly comparable with drawing to an inside straight at Poker. The man who says, "Never draw to an inside straight," overstates the case, and so does the man who says, "Never speculate at Gin." But it is a better case than Cowboy's.

The arguments in favor of speculation are:

1) It increases the chances of building a set.

2) It may help salvage a bad hand.

3) It may open a new avenue for a hand which has reached a dead end.

4) It may cause the other player to ruin his hand by holding on to cards he cannot use except to block the speculator.

5) There may be a future pay-off; the other player may come to suspect speculation where there is none.

The arguments against speculation are :

1) The increased chances of building a set are overbalanced by the loss of a pick from the stock. Usually only a few picks are available before somebody knocks, and each pick is an opportunity which should not be wasted.

2) The speculator gives away too much information; he eases the pressure on the other player.

3) Speculation does not succeed often enough to be profitable over the long haul.

Presented this way in print, the issue may seem to be closer than it really is. Speculation at Gin seldom pays. To help evaluate it, let us consider typical situations.

At regular Gin where the knock is ten, suppose you hold:

♠	♡	◇		♣	♣		♡	◇		♣	♡	♠
Q	Q	Q		9	8		7	7		5	3	2

Certainly this is a promising hand. Two perfect picks would enable you to knock, and any one of many cards can help you immediately by extending your set of Q's, or building one of your combinations into a set, or reducing your unrelated deadwood. Your opponent discards the ♠5, and you see in a flash that it would give you a third combination. But you don't need that combination, and there is no card you can afford to give up for the ♠5. Even Potzer would refuse it.

Suppose your opponent discards instead the ♣2. Picking it would combine speculation with a reduction in your deadwood, but would still be a poor choice, for you would be giving away too much in terms of time. Your object should be to build one of your higher card combinations into a set as soon as possible. You cannot afford to play for a set of 2's, and delay trying to catch a card which will match your ♣9 8, or two 7's. Potzer might see the situation in another light; the lowness of the ♣2 might lure him.

But suppose your opponent discards instead the ◊6. Now even a stronger player than Potzer might pick it, because it would double the chances of completing a set in the area of the 7's. At the same time, however, picking the ◊6 would mean by-passing an opportunity for immediate improvement in the hand. The percentage is against picking the ◊6, and by a substantial margin.

There is no speculation which can be justified with so good a hand, but suppose you have just dealt yourself a horrible one, as follows:

♠	♡	◊	♣	♠	♡	◊	♣	♡	♣
K	Q	J	10	9	8	8	6	5	4

If there is any consolation, it is that your opponent probably holds a hand which is not much better, but you cannot count on that. Only one of the two outstanding 8's can immediately build a set for you, and you long for more chances. Your opponent gives them to you by discarding the ◊7. If you should pick it, you would treble your chances of completing a set: in addition to the two outstanding 8's, either of the two outstanding 7's, or the ◊9 or ◊6 could complete a set for you. The speculation would be reasonable — because of the inferior quality of your hand.

Consider now a situation late in the play. You hold:

♠	♡	♡	◇	◇	◇	♠	♡	◇	♣
J	J	10	9	8	7	5	4	3	A

The hand has remained top-heavy because you have been forced to unload unrelated picture cards. Your opponent discards the ♡3, and you know he would not have parted with so low a card unless he were close to knocking. You should seriously consider speculating: picking the ♡3, and discarding your ♠J or ♡10. Unless at least three cards in the J J 10 area are live, and if at least two cards in the 4 3 3 area are live, you should pick the ♡3. It is time for a switch and deadwood reduction.

Whatever the game, you will find among its devotees the man who would rather win by deception than by constructive effort. At Chess he sets traps at the expense of position; at Bridge he puts in psychic bids; at Gin he bluffs with picks in no way related to anything he holds.

As a sort of practical joke, Cowboy enjoys a bluff at Gin. Kibitz him with this hand:

♡	◇	♣	♠	♠	♠	♡	♣	♡	◇
10	10	10	9	8	7	6	6	3	2

Cautious discards the ♣5. Cowboy grabs it, discards the ♡3, and says, "Bless your little heart."

For a moment Cautious is flabbergasted. He was sure the ♣5 was a safe discard, and he now recapitulates. Yes, Cowboy is bluffing. Cautious picks, and scornfully discards another 5. "Bless your big heart," Cautious says.

Deciding that the joke has gone far enough, Cowboy makes a serious pick, and discards the ♣5.

Cautious grins. "Smoked you out, didn't I!"

"Just play the game," Cowboy says.

Cautious plays it by picking from the stock, and knocking.

Potzer, who was silent during the play, says, "That was some bluff."

"It didn't exactly pan out," Cowboy says, "but did you happen to notice the expression on Cautious's puss when I glommed onto the ♣5?"

"It cost you a few points," Cautious says.

"It was a bargain," Cowboy says.

If you can get laughs out of losing, bluffing at Gin may be one way. Otherwise, it has no merit. The risk is out of proportion to the remotely possible gain.

CHAPTER 9

Starting play

As you arrange your original hand, you spontaneously give it some kind of quality rating. You do not necessarily put the thought into words; you do not say to yourself, "This hand is glorious," or, "This hand is miserable." Your reaction is largely emotional; you experience a feeling of elation, confidence, hope, determination, chagrin or despair, according to your cards and your temperament. Emotion soon gives way to cerebration. You begin to calculate. You evaluate your chances, and formulate a plan.

Your hand may be excellent; it may offer so many opportunities for an early knock that your first play becomes automatic, with little or no concern for what your opponent may try to do. Your hand may be so bad, so disparate, that you have no sensible choice except to start unloading your high-count deadwood. But most original hands belong in some category between these extremes; most hands range from good to poor.

Since the odds are against catching a set in the original hand, many players generalize that any original hand which contains a set must be rated good. If you accept this, you will soon encounter enough exceptions to make the generalization meaningless. For the time being, think only of regular Gin where the knock is ten, and compare these three hands:

(I)   ♠   ♡   ◇   ♣   ♡   ♣   ♠   ♡   ◇   ♣
     K   Q   J   10   8   7   5   A   A   A

(II)   ♡ ♡   ♠ ♡ ♣   ♢ ♣ ♠ ♡ ♣
      K Q   10 10 10   6 4 3 2 A

(III) ♡ ♢ ♣   ♡ ♡   ♢ ♣ ♠ ♡ ♣
      K K K   8 7   J 4 3 2 A

Although there is a set in each of these hands, brief analysis will show distinct quality differences among them. Putting them into one large, amorphous category can have little significance.

In example I, despite the presence of the set of A's the over-all pattern is poor. You need a pick to build a combination, and then a perfect pick to build a second set. Even if you soon build a second set, your high-count deadwood will prevent you from knocking. If your opponent can soon knock, your high-count deadwood will be expensive to you.

In example II, and similarly in example III, one perfect pick will build a second set, and you will then be able to knock. Obviously the number of perfect picks needed for going down is a better measure of quality than whether the original hand contains a set. Examples II and III are *one-pick hands,* but they do not offer you the same chances. For a more precise evaluation, you must consider the number of chances.

In example II only one outstanding card, the ♡J, can immediately build a second set. You have here a *one-pick hand with one chance.*

In example III either of two outstanding cards, the ♡9 or ♡6, can immediately build a second set. You have here a *one-pick hand with two chances.* At this stage, example III is twice as good as example II, and both are much better than example I.

Compare the foregoing with this hand:

(IV) ♢ ♡ ♡ ♣ ♣ ♠ ♠   ♡ ♢ ♣
      8 8 7 7 6 6 5   2 2 A

Although it contains no set, it is replete with combinations. Any outstanding 8 or 7 or 6 — or the ♡9 — or the ♣5 — or the ♠4 — or either outstanding 2 — will build a set. They add up to eleven chances to build a set, and if you catch in the intermediate area you will be approaching an early knock. This hand is excellent.

Let us go down the scale for one more comparison. Here is about as bad a hand as you can hold:

(V)   ♠   ♣   ♡   ♠   ◇   ♣   ♡   ◇   ♣   ♡
      K   Q   J   10   9   8   7   6   5   4

There is not even one combination, and the outlook is dismal. Can any procedure bring it up from the category of the hopeless? Perhaps.

Let us go back, take the examples in order, and do some planning.

Holding example I, you should forthwith try to unload some of your high-count deadwood, and try to catch one more set. If you catch a good knock cache, you may then be able to go down; otherwise you may have to play for a third set — if your opponent gives you the time.

Holding example II, your plan will depend on the first card you pick. If the long shot comes in — if your opponent discards the ♡J, or if you pick it from the stock — you will knock, and probably enter a big score. If your first pick is a K or Q, you should discard the ◇6, and hope for the best. If your first pick is an unrelated picture card, or a 10, or a 9, discarding it will be the least of the evils. If your first pick is an 8 or lower card, your best course will be to discard the K.

Holding example III, your course will be clear. You will play with a view to catching a second set and going down at the earliest opportunity.

Holding example IV, your course will be less clear, for you may find yourself suffering from an excess of wealth. Suppose you catch the ♡6. You will have to decide whether to hold the ♡ sequence or the set of 6's. Such situations will be analyzed in succeeding chapters; meanwhile you should stay on offense, looking to improvement of your hand.

Examples I to IV have ranged from poor to excellent. In each case, the plan has consisted in offense. You will find some such initial plan suitable for most of the hands dealt to you.

Holding a hand such as example V, you may find it expedient to go on defense for a while, trying to thwart your opponent by refusing to release any card he may be able to use. It amounts to a delaying action tinged with desperation. Nobody enjoys defense which, if prolonged, can lead to a stand-off at best.

"An expert shows his greatest skill when he defends," Cautious says.

"Where's the profit in defense?" Cowboy asks.

"Defense is definitely a question mark," Clipper says.

On the average, you will be forced to go on defense with your original hand less than ten percent of the time.

At Oklahoma Gin, early planning is materially influenced by the upcard. Thirty-one percent of the time, the upcard is a K, Q, J or 10, so there is no difference. Fifteen percent of the time, the upcard is a 9 or 8, and the difference is slight. The planning may be similar if the upcard is a 7 or 6 for a knock cache of four cards is still possible, although more difficult to accumulate.

If the upcard is a 5 or lower, the planning must change markedly. Examination of the table which follows will show why this is so.

MAXIMUM KNOCK CACHES AT OKLAHOMA GIN

Upcard	Number of Cards	Kinds
K, Q, J or 10	5	4 2 2 A A 3 3 2 A A
9	5	3 2 2 A A
8	4	4 2 A A 3 3 A A 3 2 2 A
7	4	3 2 A A
6	4	2 2 A A
5	3	3 A A 2 2 A
4	3	2 A A
3	2	2 A
2	2	A A
A	0	You must play for Gin

When the upcard is anything from a K to a 9, you can knock by melding five cards, one long sequence. Melding two three-card sets is more usual.

As you go down the line, the operation becomes progressively more difficult. A glance at the table shows why: the maximum knock caches become progressively shorter, or the possible kinds become fewer, or they become shorter and fewer. The minimum melds become progressively longer.

When the upcard is an 8 or 7 or 6, you must meld at least six cards.

When the upcard is a 5 or 4, you must meld at least seven cards.

When the upcard is a 3 or 2, you must meld at least eight cards.

When the upcard is an A, you must go Gin, melding ten cards.

Let us now go back to examples of hands I to V, and formulate a plan for each at Oklahoma Gin when the upcard is a 5 or lower.

Example I is relatively better, because you are likely to gain time. Fundamentally, your plan is unchanged, but you can afford to proceed with more daring.

Example II is also relatively better. You can afford to hold your K Q combination longer. If you pick another K or Q, you can afford to hold your overlapping sequences for a while.

Example III is no longer a one-pick hand. You must extend one of your two sets and reduce your knock cache; you should try to build a third set. Meanwhile, your opponent may go ahead of you; you may have to defend.

Example IV stands up well. If the upcard is a 5, your knock cache is adequate, and you can go down by melding seven cards. If the upcard is a 4, your prospects for an early knock remain bright. If the upcard is a 3 or 2 or A, you should play for gin; you figure to beat your opponent to it.

Example V offers more hope than it did at regular Gin. Here unless your opponent holds a phenomenal hand, time will be your ally. While you do not figure to win, your losing margin is unlikely to be so great, and there is a better chance that the tide will turn. You should start cautiously, defending wherever necessary; you should go on offense as soon as you have caught a set or two combinations.

When you are the non-dealer at Oklahoma Gin, your advantage is increased by the first option on the upcard.

If the upcard completes a set, you will always pick it.

If the upcard extends a set, you will *almost* always pick it. The rare exception is the type of hand where extending a set would compel you to break up a combination. For example:

♠	♡	◇	♣		♠	♠	♠		♠	♣	♣
Q	Q	Q	Q		10	9	8		5	5	4

This is the type of hand with which you should play for Gin — a one-pick hand with four chances to that end. Suppose the upcard is the ♠7. If you pick it, what will you discard? Any discard from your overlapping combinations — from the 5 5 4 — will reduce your chances by fifty percent.

When the upcard is an A, many players pick it mechanically, forgetting that it makes the knock Gin. The A should be picked only when it completes or extends a set, and never on speculation. There is little to fear in refusing it; the K and A are the cards least likely to be constructive in the other player's hand.

In some circles, regular Gin is played with an upcard, but remember that the knock is always ten. There the A should usually be picked as a reducer. The 2 is also a good reducer.

The 3 is a borderline card; it is useful as a reducer in some cases. For example:

♠	♡	♣		♢	♢	♢		♣		♠	♡	♢
9	9	9		5	4	3		2		K	Q	J

Any 3 here is a good pick. The ♣3 is especially valuable, for it simultaneously reduces the deadwood and forms a combination.

Now study this example:

♠	♡	♢		♡	♠	♠		♠	♡	♢	♣
9	9	9		6	6	5		K	Q	J	2

No 3 is a good pick here. With only one set, you should pick from the stock, hoping to build a second set.

If your hand is full of strangers, picking an intermediate or low upcard on speculation may be advisable. Suppose you hold example V, and the upcard is the ♣7 or ♡6. With a hand so barren, you should pick it, for it will give your four chances to build a set. Discarding the K, you will also reduce your deadwood count.

A desperation measure with example V would be to bluff by picking an upcard which does not form a combination.

The idea: to mislead your opponent — to induce him to hold on to cards which would combine with your pick but cannot combine with anything he holds. It is an idea with a better chance of success against an imaginative player than a plodder or an inattentive one. If you try it against Potzer, he will play without regard for it; he is oblivious to real hazards, so there is no reason to believe he will develop visual powers in the face of a spurious one. If you try it against Wander, he may promptly forget the suit, and then the rank.

Like all other bluffs, this one can boomerang. Playing against Wander, Cowboy holds:

$$\begin{array}{cccc@{\quad}cc@{\quad}cccc} \heartsuit & \spadesuit & \diamondsuit & \clubsuit & \diamondsuit & \heartsuit & \spadesuit & \clubsuit & \diamondsuit & \heartsuit \\ K & Q & J & 9 & 7 & 7 & 6 & 5 & 4 & 2 \end{array}$$

The upcard is the ♠10, in which there is no nourishment Cowboy decides he can profit more in the long run by adding to Wander's confusion than by trying immediately to improve his own hand. It will be more fun, too. He picks the ♠10, discards the ♡K, registers satisfaction.

Wander's mind is partly on the game tonight. He holds:

$$\begin{array}{cc@{\quad}cc@{\quad}cc@{\quad}cccc} \diamondsuit & \clubsuit & \spadesuit & \heartsuit & \spadesuit & \diamondsuit & \diamondsuit & \heartsuit & \spadesuit & \clubsuit \\ K & K & J & 10 & 8 & 8 & 6 & 5 & 3 & A \end{array}$$

Since Wander holds the ♠J and 8, he knows Cowboy cannot hold a ♠ sequence — evidently he holds 10's. Wander picks the K, discards the ♠J.

Cowboy begins to lose faith in his bluff. He picks the ♣6 from the stock, discards the ♠Q.

Wander picks the ♣8, discards the ♡10 — remembers suddenly that Cowboy had picked the ♠10, and nearly panics as he wishes he could retract the play.

Disgustedly Cowboy picks from the stock, discards the ♠10.

Wander is astonished. "Wasn't that the upcard?"

"Uhuh." Cowboy dolefully contemplates his hand.

"That's what I thought." Wander picks the ◊A, and knocks.

A kibitzer slaps Wander on the back. "Couldn't fool you, could he!"

"Naaa," Wander says. "I was hep all the way."

CHAPTER 10

Discards

Part of the non-dealer's initial advantage evaporates when he makes his first discard, for it is the only completely blind play in the hand. Of course, he selects for the purpose a card which is not part of a set, and normally not part of a combination. If he is an inexperienced player, he may consider rank to the exclusion of other factors. Holding a lone K but lacking the Q of the same suit, he discards the K. Otherwise he goes down the line, discarding the Q or J or 10. He reasons that he is reducing his deadwood, and often bypasses a better discard. Among experienced players, there are many who stay in the same rut.

If your original hand is poor, you should consider as your first discard a very *low* card. Suppose you hold after your first pick:

♠	♡	♠	◇	♡	♣	♠	♡	♣	◇	♠
Q	10	9	9	8	7	6	5	4	2	A

Although the Q may appear to be your best discard because it is useless and has a count of ten, your 2 is no more likely to help your opponent build a set. If you discard your 2, and if he picks it to build a set of 2's or a 3 2 A set, he will have reduced very little. He may reason that, if you can afford to part with so low a card, you must be strong in the intermediate or high areas. He may then dream up "defenses" which help you, and hinder him in the development of his hand.

Except where a 2 is part of a set, strong combination or knock cache, it is usually as good a blind discard as a Q, and better than a J or 10. With a bad hand, you may find it advantageous even to discard a lone A.

When the choice of discards boils down to one of several in the same area, the first minor mistake is often made. Suppose you hold after your first pick:

♡	♠	♡	♠	◇	♣	♣	♠	◇	♡	♣
J	10	9	8	8	6	5	4	3	2	A

Check the suits closely, lest you mechanically discard the ♡J. If you do that, and if your next pick is the ♡10, you will regret your haste. True, the chance of catching the ♡10 is remote, but you owe yourself that chance, and your first discard should be the ♠10. There is salesmanship as well as percentage in it: if your opponent holds the ♡10, he may blithely give it to you. Don't discourage him from doing so.

I am sure you will not construe this as advice to hold on to broken sequences except where other factors are approximately equal. If in the foregoing situation, after you have discarded the ♠10, your opponent discards the ♠2, and you pick the ♡6, you should unload the ♡J.

Your first turn to play may give you the opportunity to send forth an intermediate or low card entirely for selling purposes. Suppose you hold:

♡	♠	♡	◇	♣	♠	◇	♠	♣	◇
Q	J	9	9	7	6	6	3	2	2

You pick the ♠A which gives you a long knock cache. Your useless cards are the ♡Q, ♠J and ♣7. If you discard the Q or J you will have unloaded some of your high-count deadwood, but discarding the 7 is a much better play. Your opponent may think you are trying to lure him into discarding a 7 in another suit. He will surely reason that you are not breaking up a 7 6 combination. If he holds a lone 6, he may consider that a safe discard — one that is unlikely to build a set in your hand. This presupposes that he has some knowledge of Gin strategy; against an inept opponent your best discard is probably the Q or J.

If your original hand is top-heavy, that is, if it contains a preponderance of ten-count cards, begin to unload some of them, even at the expense of combinations. Suppose you hold:

♡	♡	◇	◇	♣	♠	◇	♣	♠	♣
K	Q	Q	J	J	6	6	6	3	A

If your pick is a 7 or lower, you should discard the K. If your next pick is a 7 or lower, you should discard the ♡Q. Such unloading is doubly advisable at "spades double."

The dealer's first play is not entirely blind. Whatever the non-dealer's first discard, it conveys some information — information which may be immediately pertinent or may become pertinent later. Suppose you are the dealer and hold:

♣	♡	♠	◇	♡	♣	♠	◇	◇	♡
Q	J	9	8	7	6	4	4	3	2

Your opponent's first discard is the ♣9. You pick the ♠5. All of your cards from the 6 up are useless, and you want to determine which is the safest discard. Let us consider your cards in descending order, with the ♣9 staring up at us from the table.

The Q and J are wild; there is no evidence that your opponent cannot use them, and a slight indication that he can. The lack of picture cards in your hand suggests that your opponent holds a few in that area — you cannot be sure, but you need not discard your Q or J to find out. You assume that your opponent has not discarded from a combination: he does not hold another 9, or the ♣10, or the ♣8. Your ♠9 may appear to be a safe discard, but at this early stage the ♣9 may be a salesman; your opponent may hold the ♠J 10, or the ♠8 7. In short, he may be perpetrating a legitimate swindle, so your logical discard is the ◇8 or ♣6. You should select the ◇8 because of its higher count.

This play carries out an important principle: where you lack more definite information, your safest discard is likely to be in a rank which *adjoins* your opponent's last discard, and *in another suit*.

Suppose you have discarded the ◇8 as recommended, and your opponent now discards the ◇9. Obviously it is the card he has just picked, and his hand is unchanged. Unless you pick a card which combines with your ♣6, the 6 should be your next discard.

But be careful in applying this principle against an expert. If he knows that you know it, he may bait you accordingly.

Continuing with the play of this hand, suppose you now pick the ♣A, and discard the ♣6. He refuses it, picks from the stock, discards the ♣5. You pick the ♣4, and your hand now is:

♣	♡	♠	♡	♠	♠	♣	◇	◇	♡	♣
Q	J	9	7	5	4	4	4	3	2	A

Although your opponent has played only three times, you already know much about his hand. He holds no 9's. He probably does not hold two 8's or two 6's, because if he had just picked and 8 or 6 he would probably have discarded it in preference to the lower count 5. He has probably caught several ten-count cards along the way, and his unwillingness to part with any of them indicates that they are in sets or combinations. Therefore:

Your safest discard is the 9; you cannot afford to part with your 2 or A lest it enable him to knock. You must hope that you will catch cards which will enable you to do something constructive in the low area. Meanwhile, your opponent may begin unloading high-count cards, making it safe for you to discard your Q and J. A little analysis coupled with a little patience will have paid off to you.

When you pick your opponent's discard to complete a set,

he may be in the dark as to whether it is in one rank or a
sequence. Try to keep him in the dark as long as possible.
Suppose you hold:

♡	◇		♠	♣		◇	◇	◇		♠	♠	♡
K	K		Q	9		8	7	6		5	4	A

Your opponent discards the ♠K which you pick. This is
not the time to say a quick farewell to your useless ♠Q which
will immediately scream to your opponent that you hold
K's. Unless you know he needs the ♣9, let that be your discard, for there is a difference of only one point in the count,
and in this situation even a greater point difference would
be less important than withholding information from him.

You may catch an original hand which is promising, only
to be forced back on defense after a few plays. At Oklahoma
Gin, suppose you have just dealt yourself:

♣	♣	◇		◇	◇	◇		♡	♡		♠	♣
K	Q	K		J	10	9		7	7		3	3

The upcard is the ◇Q. While you look hungrily at it, your
opponent picks it. You hope he is bluffing, realize that he
probably isn't, and mark time as he discards the ♣8.

You pick the ♡10, inspect it, discard it.

He dives for the ♡10, discards the ♣2. It is now evident
that his high-card picks have been for improvement — that
he holds either a long ♡ sequence, or sets of Q's and 10's.

You pick the ♡3, discard the ◇K which is probaly safe.

He picks from the stock, discards the ◇6.

You pick the ◇3, discard the ♣K which is almost certainly
safe.

He picks from the stock, discards the ♠6.

You pick the ◇8 and would like to hold it, but you cannot
afford the luxury. If you discard the ♣Q, it may enable him
to knock. Surely you will not break up your 7's or 3's. So
you must defend. You discard the ◇8; you hold on to your
useless ♣Q to block your opponent.

In the chapter headed *Choices and Chances,* it was dem-
onstrated that the K's and A's can be used four ways to build
three-card sets, the Q's and 2's five ways, and the other cards
six ways for that purpose. As soon as the first discard goes
on the pile, it decreases the number of ways in which cards
in the area can be used to build sets. Suppose you hold:

♡	♠	◇	♡	♠	♣	♣	♡	♠	◇
Q	J	J	9	8	7	6	5	4	3

Your opponent discards the ♠9. Unless you pick it on
speculation, a poor play, you know that your ♠8 can now
be used only four ways, for the ♠10 9 8 and 9 8 7 sequences
become impossible.

The effect of a discard on the pertinent chances may be
less obvious, so that you must use your powers of deduction
to bring them into focus. Suppose you hold the same hand,
and your opponent discards instead the ♣9. Do you see how
it affects your ♠8?

You start by assuming that your opponent has not broken
a combination of 9's. Since he does not hold the ♠9, he cannot use your ♠8 to build the ♠10 9 8 or 9 8 7 sequence. He
can use your ♠8 only four ways: three ways to build a set
of 8's, and one way to build a sequence, the ♠8 7 6. Your 8
is a safer discard than your Q.

The proximity of combinations may reduce the number
of chances. Suppose your hand contains:

♣	♣	♡	◇
J	10	9	9

A superficial estimate of your chances in this area may
erroneously add up to four. If you look closely, you will see
that your chances add up to only three, for the ♣9 will build
either the ♣J 10 9 sequence or a set of 9's. Therefore you
should regard either the ♣J 10 or the two 9's as a one-chance
combination as long as both combinations remain in your
hand. Your best discard may be from one of these, if the rest

of your cards are in sets, combinations or a knock cache. The 10 or one of the 9's may be a good salesman, too. If you discard the ♣10, your opponent may give you a 9. If you discard one of your 9's, he may give you the ♣9.

There is always a risk in sending out a salesman: your opponent may hire him.

Throughout the game, keep in mind your opponent's quirks. These are common:

Holding on to low cards even when they are useless;

Holding on to high card combinations into the last stages;

Frequent speculation;

Superstitiously refusing to part with any card of a certain rank.

I know a player who persistently saves 7's and 3's, no matter how useless. He insists that his luck is bad, but his system of logic counsels no change in this practice.

CHAPTER **11**

The late rounds

Any round after the fifth is late because it has carried play beyond the average number of picks. Potzer and Cautious, opponents tonight, have reached such a round. Potzer has developed a hand which fills him with an uneasy kind of hope: he knows he is close to Gin; he believes Cautious is also close to it. Potzer holds:

♠	♡	♣	♡	♡	♡	♣	♣	♣	♡
Q	Q	Q	9	8	7	8	7	6	4

Potzer had thought of knocking at his previous turn, but had desisted for fear of an undercut. Now he picks the ♣2, thinks again of knocking, remembers vaguely that Cautious holds a 2 which may be a loner. Potzer decides to go for Gin. He discards the ♡4, which Cautious refuses. The refusal is a reprieve for Potzer: two rounds ago he discarded the ♣4, and Cautious picked it. As Cautious takes a card from the stock and goes into a trance, Potzer's optimism mounts. Potzer's estimate of his chances is five: the ♢Q or ♡10 or ♣9 or ♣5 will do the job. The estimate bears no relation to reality.

Early in the play, three K's in succession hit the discard pile, and Cautious picked one of them. It was the ♢K, and obviously built a sequence which includes the ♢Q. Potzer gave that no consideration.

Before Potzer began building his ♡ sequence, he discarded the ♡10, and Cautious discarded the ♡6. There can

be no extension of that sequence, but Potzer has forgotten
those discards.

Potzer has forgotten also that when he picked the ♡9 to
build his ♡ sequence, he discarded the ♣9.

That leaves one live card, the ♣5, for Potzer. But how live
is it? Cautious, holding the ♣4, refused the ♡4. The ♣4 must
be part of a sequence which could be the 6 5 4 or 5 4 3 or
4 3 2. Roughly the odds are two to one that Cautious holds
the ♣5. So at best Potzer has one-third of one chance of going Gin.

Nevertheless Potzer is undaunted. As far as he is concerned, the hand has developed into a race in which either
he or Cautious will be "lucky." But it is a race in which the
odds heavily favor Cautious, who does remember most of the
previous action and has accurately analyzed it. If Potzer
realized how badly he is hobbled, he would halt the race
by knocking; then he might be undercut, but Cautious's
bonus would be no greater than for going Gin. It is not certain that Cautious could undercut Potzer; it is practicably
certain that if play continues Cautious will go Gin.

The hand points up one of the most delicate problems of
the late rounds: *when to try for Gin.* Only the player who
remembers and understands the previous action can decide
logically. He must ask himself:

1) Can I go down without being undercut?

2) As closely as I have been able to calculate my chances
of going Gin, what are they?

3) If I can't go down, what can I do to block my opponent?

If an undercut appears certain, the idea of going down
short of Gin must, of course, be abandoned. *If an undercut
is not certain, the best policy usually is to knock at the first
opportunity.* This policy will win more points than it loses
over a series of sessions.

Theoretically the ideal hand with which to go for Gin
needs only one pick with nine chances, and contains an un-

matched A. It is rare; only one hundred and thirty-two hands of this type are possible. An example:

♠	♠	♠	♡	♡	♡	♣	♣	♣	♢
8	7	6	8	7	6	8	7	6	A

The unmatched A guarantees that the other player will be undercut if he goes down short of Gin. Remember that if he does so and is tied it is an undercut.

In actual play such a hand seldom offers the maximum number of chances. By the time three such pliable sets have been built, some of the cards which could extend one of them have been picked by the other player or lie buried in the discard pile.

A dozen or a thousand dozen hands with many chances for Gin in one pick could be set down, but they would be mere abstractions if lifted out of the context of play to the stage where they had been accumulated. Consider the ideal nine-chance hand used as an illustration. If the other player held a set of four 9's, the chances would drop to six. If a 5 had been discarded by you and picked by him in the early going — but why go on? The *live* chances are those which matter. A rule of thumb about as satisfactory as any in the late rounds is:

Holding a one-pick hand with four or more live chances for Gin, try for it if you have reason to believe a knock short of Gin will be undercut.

Be alert for opportunities to increase your chances by re-arranging your hand. Suppose you hold:

♡	♡	♡	♣	♣	♣	♣	♠	♡	♡
Q	J	10	J	10	9	8	4	4	3

You need one of the two outstanding 4's or the ♡5 or ♡2 to go Gin — four chances — but suppose the 2's are dead, and the live chances total only three. You pick the ♠5. If the ♠6 and ♠3 are live, and if the ♡3 is safe, discard the 3. In this case you will not only have added to your chances by rearranging your combination, but also the discarded 3 may function as a salesman. To a strong opponent, the pitch will not be very convincing, but it will be a minor plus none-theless.

Inevitably you will find yourself in situations where you have no safe discard, and the choice is between a high or intermediate and a low card. Suppose you must discard an 8 or a 4, and you know that either will build a set in your opponent's hand. Give him the lower card. Suppose he holds:

♠	♡	◇	♣	♡	◇	♠	◇	♡	♣
K	K	K	K	8	8	4	4	3	2

If you give him the 8, he may discard a 4 and knock. By giving him the 4, you leave him with the task of building a set of 8's, and a deadwood count of nineteen or eighteen depending on whether he discards the 3 or 2. Even if he breaks the 8's he cannot knock.

When you have the unhappy choice of two discards, one of which will extend a set in your opponent's hand, while the other will build a new set for him, make the discard which will extend the set. Suppose your choice has narrowed down to the ♠9 or ♡7, and he holds:

♠	♠	♠	◇	♣	♣	♠	♠	♡	♡
Q	J	10	7	7	6	5	4	3	A

Giving him the ♠9 will not help his immediate chances, whereas giving him the 7 will move him a long way toward a knock.

Painful though it may be, you may have to decline the opportunity to extend a set in your hand — you may even have to break up a set to block your opponent. In a late round, suppose you hold:

♠	♠	♠	♡	◇	♣	♠	♠	♡	◇
Q	J	10	8	8	8	6	5	4	3

From the early action, you know your opponent holds ♡

CHAPTER 12

Team play

Last Saturday night there was a party at Cowboy's home. Proteus was invited but had a previous engagement. Today they take lunch together. Cowboy says, "You should've been there. After dinner the men organized a team game, six against six. What a brawl."

"While I'm sorry I missed your party, I cannot honestly say the same about the team jamboree." Proteus spears the olive in his martini. "As far as I'm concerned, Gin is a solo game. Why spoil it?"

"A team game can be a barrel of fun. The craziest things happen." Cowboy chuckles. "Take Wander . . ."

"I'm tired of taking him," Proteus cuts in. "I have a conscience."

Cowboy insists on telling what Wander did. "He forgot which team he was on, and misread the score. He played accordingly — took a long chance which didn't come off. Did he gum things up!"

"Is that sort of thing an inducement?"

"It was amusing."

"To Wander's partners?"

"Hardly. Cautious blew a gasket."

"That's what I mean." Proteus takes a sip. "When I'm at a party where the majority want to play team against team, I ride along. Where I have a choice, I prefer to be strictly on my own."

"Team play is an enjoyable change. A real challenge,

and ◊ sequences in the low area. You pick the ♠K. Parting with your 4 or 3 would be foolhardy, so you discard the K.

Suppose you hold:

♠	♡	♣	◊	◊	◊	◊	♡	♣	♠
J	J	J	J	9	8	7	6	6	5

You know your opponent holds three 3's, and needs only a little improvement to knock. You pick the ♠3 which you cannot aford to give him, so you discard a J. If your opponent improves his hand from the stock and knocks, you will have added only three points to your deadwood total.

Where both players must go for Gin, repeated blocking of this kind may become necessary down to the last two cards. Players who cannot bring themselves to sacrifice sets or combinations for the sake of a stand-off might do well to meditate on an ancient method of trapping monkeys. A tidbit is put into a heavy jar with a neck just wide enough to permit a monkey to stick an arm inside. The jar is left under a tree. A monkey comes along, reaches into the jar, wraps a first around the tidbit, tries to pull it out. The fist is too big to pass through. All the monkey has to do to escape is let go, but he is stubborn. He soon finds himself in the hunter's sack.

too. You've got to modify your strategy and tactics."

"That's what most Gin players think." Proteus nibbles a potato chip. "I dissent. Good gin is good Gin, and bad Gin is bad Gin, whether one man opposes one, two oppose two or more oppose more. No matter how many are on each side, a team game remains a series of individual contests. In the main, it's the same, with more bookkeeping."

"There's got to be a difference."

"Yes, there's one big difference." Proteus's tone could etch steel. "At team play I'm often axed by a palooka partner. I beat my brains out to win ten points on a hand, and he blows fifty. The essential winning tactics is to cut away from somebody like Potzer."

Cowboy winces at the memory of Potzer as a partner, rallies to his defense. "Potzer is an amiable guy."

"Who said he isn't?"

"It's the same for everybody when there's a weak man." Cowboy orders another martini, drier.

Proteus orders another martini not so dry. "So is smallpox the same for everybody, but why expose oneself to it?"

"That's a harsh analogy. What's more, smallpox is not the same for everybody. Some people recover from it, some don't."

Proteus laughs. "You've made the analogy perfect."

"With or without analogies, I enjoy both individual and team Gin. I've learned to make the necessary adjustments."

Proteus folds his arms across his chest. "Such as?"

"Well, at team play it's paramount to get on score as soon as possible."

"What's wrong with that idea when you're on your own?"

"Nothing, absolutely nothing, but at team play you've got the others on your side to consider."

"A noble sentiment. If team play makes people a little less selfish, I heartily approve."

Cowboy emphasizes his point: "You've got to do everything within your power to avert a blitz."

"Since the object is to win, I should think you'd always be aware of the possibility of a blitz until both individuals or sides get on score." Proteus assumes his courtroom manner. "I am under the impression that a blitz always doubles the score. Correct me if I'm wrong."

"Oh, you're absolutely right. Nevertheless it's more important to avert a blitz when you've got a partner."

"Why?"

"Well, now — in a — I mean you . . ." Cowboys pauses to reassemble his thoughts. "It just is," he blurts out.

"The evidence up to this point leaves me unconvinced."

Cowboy fumbles in his brain for evidence. The second martini does not help him find it. "At team play it is usually advisable to knock as early as possible."

"I'm an early knock man myself. Give me a sound reason for any other policy when you're on your own."

Cowboy is squirming under the examination. "You know what I mean. It's a sort of extra obligation when you're a member of a team. I modify my style somewhat — tighten up my game."

"Have you considered that modification at your solo games? As a friend, may I call to your attention that you'd save money?"

"Maybe so." Cowboy does not want to discuss his tactics at solo play. "In a team game, when you're dealt a lousy hand, you've got to unload your picture cards and 10's, 9's too, as fast as possible. You're going to take a shellacking, so lighten the burden on your partner."

"With a similar hand at solo play, doesn't it make sense to follow the same procedure, so as to lighten the subsequent burden on yourself? I can't see how the idea of unloading from a bad hand is unique to team play."

Cowboy is stubborn. "Maybe it isn't, but there is a difference. I could show you plenty of hands to prove it."

"Show me one."

With a ball point pen on a napkin, Cowboy writes:

♡ ♡ ♠ ♡ ♣ ◇ ♡ ♠ ◇ ♠
K Q 9 8 7 6 5 4 3 2

Proteus wrinkles his nose. "A stinker, anywhere in the universe."

"Cautious dealt it to me." Cowboy's tone is mournful. "If I'd been alone against him, I'd have ditched the 9. With a partner's interest also at stake, I ditched the King."

"You're proud of that?"

"Not proud. Let's say I'm well satisfied. I picked another 9 from the stock, then Cautious threw me one."

"That proves nothing. Discarding the King was questionable, especially against Cautious. For the sake of one point in your deadwood count, you broke up the only combination in your hand. Yes, I know it was a one-way combination, but Cautious always discards from the top down — you've played against him enough to realize that. I think you should have discarded your 9 first, with the hope that Cautious would discard the Jack you needed."

"Maybe you're right." Cowboy orders a third martini; Proteus has had enough. Cowboy says, "Here's another example. In the same game I dealt myself a miserable hand. The only combination in it was the 9 8 of Clubs. Cautious discarded the 9 of Hearts. If it had been a solo game, I'd have picked that 9 on speculation. As a team man I had to restrain myself."

"You want my opinion?" Proteus asks. Cowboys nods. Proteus says, "Picking the 9 on speculation would be an atrocity at solo or team play."

Cowboy decided against trying to justify such speculation. "There are many situations where you must play to the team score. For instance, my partner has just been beaten by twenty points. I can go down with about six. My opponent has picked a couple of my discards — I know he holds at least two spreads, and I'll catch him for only a few points. To save the box, I'm forced to try for Gin. Wouldn't you reason the same way?"

"In such a situation I would. You've presented your first valid argument."

Cowboy feels happier. "At team play, I often take long chances when my side is running behind."

"You take them regardless."

"At team play there's justification."

"Long chances seldom come in."

"When they come in, they help the whole team." Cowboy takes a gulp.

"Over the long pull, they probably hurt the team more than they help it."

"Everybody else plays that way, too."

Proteus decides that *everybody* is too strong an antagonist. "Some traditions are sure to endure."

Cowboy ignores the irony. "I'll show you another difference. At team play you can sometimes chalk up a profit even though you lose. Suppose my partner has just knocked and won thirty points. My opponent and I are locked in a tight battle. He's got to go Gin and catch me with a deadwood count of at least six to save the box for his side. If I get my deadwood down below five, we win the box whether he Gins or not. So maybe I'll break up a combination, killing my chances of winning the hand, but cinching the box for my side."

"How about trying to block him?" Proteus calls for the check.

"Suppose you can't block him?" Cowboy grabs for the check. Proteus is quicker. They squabble for a moment, finally agree to split it. Cowboy repeats his question.

"If you can't block him, the tactic you describe is correct. I'll admit a team game presents some interesting problems, but I'll stick to my preference."

"De gustibus." Cowboy puts on his coat. "By the way, we made a new rule Saturday night. We permitted free discussion during play. Any member of a team had the right to advise any partner at any stage."

Proteus snorts. "There must have been plenty of arguments."

"Natch. But they were good natured."

"Do you know the basic strategic principle when you permit such dissemination of advice?"

Cowboy bites. "No. What is it?"

"Determine at the earliest possible moment whether your partner knows what he's talking about."

CHAPTER 13

The cheats move in

A hand is raised in the audience. Question: "Have you seen much cheating at this game?" or, "What are the common methods of cheating?" or, "How can one detect cheating?"

The subject is bound to come up during the question-and-answer session after an address on card playing. People who never touch cards ask about cheating, perhaps with the notion that I can give a sleight-of-hand performance. To many there is something titilating, something cloak-and-daggerish about the drab business of cheating. Television and radio interviewers, sensitive to what interests their public, steer discussion to it. Readers who send me letters, and strangers who call me on the telephone inquire about it — some are less concerned with self-protection than with putting the art into practice.

One evening a whining voice on the telephone asked where marked cards could be bought.

"What do you plan to do with them?"

"Tricks."

"You can learn to do plenty of tricks with ordinary cards. Get a book on magic, or take lessons from a magician."

The caller told me what he thought I ought to do; then he hung up with a bang.

Another evening, another voice. "You write that there are firms which put out catalogs of cheating equipment. Where can I get hold of such a catalog?"

"What makes you think I'd tell you?"

"Well, I'm doin' a thesis on gambling."

"At which university?"

He named a venerable one not too far away. "Don't you believe me?"

"Not yet. I'll believe you if you send me a letter furnishing some proof that you are actually working on such a thesis. Do that, and I'll see that you get a catalog."

"I'll gladly oblige you," he said.

That was over two years ago. I have not yet received the letter, and I wonder in what joints he has been earning his degree.

Is there much cheating at Gin? That depends on the place. Where any card game is played within the law, the incidence of cheating is low, in about the same proportion as at business. And it has been my experience at business that most men are trustworthy. The chiselers and deadbeats constitute a small minority, but it is a dangerous minority.

A qualification of the phrase "within the law" is necessary. The State of Connecticut in which I live has an archaic law against playing cards for money, but that does not seem to deter anybody. The people here, like Americans anywhere else, nullify any absurd law which cannot be repealed.

Incidentally, I consider Nevada's solution to the gambling problem far worse.

Where in violation of the law, an establishment exists for the purpose of playing cards for money, with the management cutting the game or charging for time, crookedness in the game is inevitable. Claiming no originality, I have counselled orally and in writing against patronizing such places. No matter how well you think you can take care of yourself at cards, you don't belong there if you are an honest man — you invite disaster when you enter.

In the last forty years, I have visited an illegal gaming establishment only once. That was in 1957, when I was working on another book and needed color. A friend provided the address and the introduction. The introduction proved to be unnecessary, for I recognized the proprietor, and he recognized me. We had played cards together elsewhere, and he had been ethical enough.

I looked about, saw some Pinochle games in progress. He said, "We'll have the kind of action you like in a little while. Gin, Poker, sit in if you're in the mood. You can do good here." I thanked him, declined, and told him my purpose. He gave me a baleful stare and said, "You mean you're going to write us up?"

"Not in a way which will help anybody identify your operation."

He asked me craftily, "Are you going to put us in a book, magazine or newspaper article?"

"I'm not going to put you anywhere. All I want is a fresh look at things."

He seemed reassured. "I'll take your word for it, but if you want to watch mechanics, you've come to the wrong place. I run honest games."

In a far corner of the room, I identified a mechanic whose acquaintance I had made twenty years earlier. "You let Puffy play here?"

The proprietor gave a high-pitched, nervous laugh. "Only Pinochle or Bridge, and with the understanding that he never shuffles, cut or deals. Anyhow, his fingers aren't what they used to be."

"So he works with a shill."

"Prove it, and I'll throw the both of them out of here. Even at that, Puffy is such a jerk that if you dealt him the Ace of Spades every time he'd still be a loser."

Before long an operator who had been barred from several decent clubs oozed in, nodded to the proprietor, made a poor job of pretending not to know me, went quickly to another room. The proprietor read me. He said, "It's a coincidence. Look, if you're going to make trouble . . ."

"I'm going to make my exit." I deemed it prudent to depart.

The card cheats fit in two major categories, each with sub categories:

1) The professionals
   (a) Full time
   (b) Part time
2) The amateurs
   (a) Abnormally greedy
   (b) Desperate
   (c) Status seeking.

The full time professionals constitute a segment of the underworld. Some use special equipment; some rely exclusively on their hands and wits. Their skills border on the miraculous. Many work with confederates.

The part time professionals are usually engaged in quasi-legitimate business, and cheat at cards to augment their incomes — or vice versa. There are more lone operators among them. Less skilled than the full time professionals, they use simpler methods.

The greedy amateurs do not ordinarily cheat out of necessity; they include people of means and high social standing. A professional man with a lucrative practice and substantial investments comes to mind. He plays for small-to-moderate stakes because he cannot bear the thought of losing at high stakes, and deals to himself from the bottom of the deck. Why does he cheat for amounts of money which cannot be significant to him? Hold on. A dime is more significant to him than it is to your bootblack.

The desperate cheats are usually neurotic gamblers who subconsciously want to lose. They cheat to get money to lose, a pathetic paradox.

Among the status seeking cheats, the money is secondary; winning is a symbol of virility. I know one who fudges strokes from his golf score even when he has no bet riding, and he has an assortment of ugly tricks at the card table. He has another quirk: to build a reputation as a horse handicapper among his friends, he sneaks to the two dollar window before a race, and buys a ticket on each entry. When the race is over, he can show a ticket on the winner. He refuses to give tips: "I don't want the responsibility."

With rare exceptions, the methods of the amateur cheats are crude.

In recent years, there has been more and more big money action at Gin — a businessman won over $300,000 at it in Florida last season — there are games where hundreds of dollars change hands in the cities and in suburbia every night. With that kind of money floating around, you would hardly expect the crooks to stay away. They are working the resorts and the ocean liners, the decent clubs and the joints, the lodges and the prosperous homes to which they can wangle invitations.

Paraphernalia used by the professional cheats includes shiners, embossing devices and marked cards. All of these are as effective at Gin as at any other game.

Shiners are reflecting devices, sometimes metal, sometimes like dentists' mirrors, by means of which the dealer can see the faces of the cards. As good a way as any to conceal a shiner is in a ring. The user of a shiner sees his victim's original hand — and remember that the winner of a hand gets to deal the next one. If your opponent is winning too consistently, and if he wears a ring, try to inspect it — and be ready to duck or block, for a shiner can inflict a nasty gash.

Embossing devices can be concealed in rings or bandages; the simplest is a small tack. The number of cards embossed need not be great to provide an enormous advantage. I have been told about two master embossers who, unknown to each other, sat down to play Gin. They used the same system, but applied it to different cards. After two hands had been completed, one of them remarked that the cards felt peculiar. A look of understanding passed between them. The winner, extending trade courtesy to the loser, made no effort to collect. They politely terminated their contest, and set out in search of non-professional opposition.

If your opponent is winning too consistently, and if you suspect an embossing job, run a hand over every card in the deck.

Every firm which supplies cheats lists standard decks with the backs so marked that the knowledgeable user can tell the rank of each card. A line is thickened here or there — a curve is broken — a small geometric figure is lightened, darkened or enlarged — so on. At least one type of marked deck which has been widely distributed makes possible identification of the suits, too. Unless you know what to look for, detection is difficult. If you have reason to believe that marked cards have found their way into your game, riffle the deck and watch for the back pattern to do a sort of shimmy. If there is no shimmy, you may be the victim of another kind of marking, detectable by means of special lenses. The face of the cheat need not be adorned by spectacles or a pince nez; thanks to modern optical science, there are contact lenses.

The cheating equipment firms also supply card marking kits, containing ink, pens and brushes for do-it-yourselfers.

Can the purveyors of such equipment be prosecuted? Ironically, no; they violate no written law, and even if some law were stretched to cover the crime, a purveyor could offer as a defense that he had in mind nothing more than the innocent pleasure of his customer.

To detect the mechanics, the sleight-of-hand artists, you need expert knowledge and excellent vision. Specialists in the field have produced clearly illustrated books which explain such manipulations, and you may find them helpful. A tip: if you suspect the opponent who gives you the deck to cut, look for a crimped card, that is, one so bent that you would naturally cut at that level. The crimp may be very small; the edge of the deck facing you may not reveal it, so pick up the deck and inspect it from every angle.

Gin lends itself to some exceedingly simple machinations — for example, the abstraction of a single card, preferably an 8 or 7 or 6, because these ranks build so many sets. The amateur is likely to sneak the abstracted card under the table. The professional will palm it and hide it somewhere on his person; he will reinsert it in the deck and will abstract another card before the next deal to allay suspicion. Suppose the missing card is the ♣6. The cheat knows that the ♣8 7 6 and 7 6 5 and 6 5 4 sequences cannot be built, and that building a set of 6's has become much more difficult. The other player may wait in vain for the ♣6, while the cheat develops a hand with which he can go Gin.

It was Chuck, a magician, who first brought to my attention the efficacy of this gimmick. To him as to others of his calling, cheating at cards is unthinkable, but he likes practical jokes. His mark was Phil, our host and a much stronger player than Chuck. Phil's quirk is a reluctance to buy new cards.

"I'm going to have some fun with him," Chuck confided to me. "Stay out of the first game."

As we sat down at the table, Phil tossed on it what he considers a new deck: a deck used only once before. "Let's cut for partners," he said.

Unlike Chuck, I dislike practical jokes, but am fascinated by his performances. I said, "I'd rather kibitz for a while."

"Suit yourself." Phil riffled the deck. They cut for deal. As Chuck cut, he abstracted the ♡7 — flashed it to me.

They played, and Chuck slaughtered Phil in a Hollywood — the last game was a blitz. Phil left the room for a moment, during which Chuck whispered to me, "I want to see if he'll catch on when I take out two cards."

Phil did not catch on.

Chuck took out a third card, and shuffled. Phil cut. They played out a hand, and again Phil lost. He assembled the cards and said, "The deck feels kind of thin."

"It's your deck," Chuck said. "Why don't you count it?"

Phil counted forty-nine cards. He fanned them out face up. "The eightaspades and the sixahearts are missing — the fivaclubs, too. Dammit, I told my wife not to let the kids play with my good cards."

"Maybe you left the missing ones in the box." Chuck registered complete innocence.

"Is this another of your lousy tricks?" Phil snapped up the lid of the box, and found the missing cards in it along with the Jokers. He drew back his arm — I intervened before he could fling the deck at Chuck.

After Phil had regained his calm, he was able to laugh. But it is not funny when a cheat shortens the deck.

Another crooked device at Gin is to leave a four-card sequence intact at the bottom of the deck — to riffle without disturbing the sequence. Suppose it is the ♠Q J 10 9. A mechanic will make sure the sequence is dealt in the original hands, the Q and 10 to his victim, the J and 9 to himself. His victim is likely soon to discard the 10: easy picking for the mechanic. An amateur can do almost as well. If the cut is deep, the sequence will be dealt in the original hands; if the cut is shallow, he has the advantage of knowing the location and order of four cards in the stock.

Watching the riffler may not be an adequate precaution. If you suspect him, insist on giving the deck a riffle yourself, and make it thorough.

It is not uncommon for a cheat to slip one unmatched card under another after a knock. "Down with four," he says blithely. His visible unmatched cards may be the ♣3 and ♠A — the ♡8 may be under the A. If he is detected, he can say, "The cards stuck together."

The remedy is as simple as the expedient: always inspect your opponent's melds, and count the cards he lays down. Don't worry about injuring his feelings. If he is honest, he will not resent your caution.

CHAPTER 14

How to remember the cards

Memory is a mysterious process. While psychiatry can explain much about what happens in the brain as it records and recalls experience, nobody knows exactly *how* it works — nobody has been able to puzzle out the mechanics by which this solid deals with the abstract things called thoughts. A California scientist recently suggested that the basis of memory lies in an increase in enzymes — we may at some future time get memory expanding doses in capsules or by hypodermic injection. Meanwhile the chemical theory, like all the others, leaves untold how the brain cells function when they remember.

Learning and memory are so intertwined as to constitute practically the same thing. Imagination is based on memory. When an artist paints a picture, he uses colors and shapes he has seen. When a scientist propounds a new theory, it is the result of his awareness of certain phenomena. When a card player conceives a new stratagem, it stems from his knowledge of the relationships between the cards and of human behavior.

The higher we move in the animal kingdom, the more the species is able to make use of recall and recognition. There is a distinction. When you pick the ♡8 from the stock, and remember that you previously discarded the ◊8 which your opponent picked, that is recall. When you see and identify the ♡8, that is recognition.

Insects cannot recall experience. Even for what appears to be recognition, they rely on instinct which may be inherited memory; they behave as their ancestors did, and learn nothing new. Their instinctive behavior compensates for the shortness of their lives: they have little time for learning.

Chimpanzees and dogs have great powers of recognition, and some recall. They can learn from experience, can be trained. Dogs have imagination, too; they dream.

Humans, of course, have the greatest powers of recall among the creatures on this planet. Among certain exceptional humans, these powers exist in a form called total recall, a kind of genius which amazes the rest. Edison could look for about a minute at a page in an unabridged dictionary, and remember everything on it. Steinmetz remembered without effort all the logarithms in his book. Gaugin would take a walk, return to his studio, and paint in detail some scene which had caught his fancy. Toscanini remembered every note in hundreds, perhaps thousands of musical compositions.

Marshall, who was the American chess champion for many years, once regaled me by replaying an entire off-hand game he had won about thirty years earlier. It was a long game with a fine, instructive ending, and I asked him why he had omitted it from his books. He answered, "I've never given it another thought until now."

All of the top-flight chess masters can play well "blindfolded," that is, without sight of the board, and so can some men below the master class. Najdorf and Koltanowski have given multiple blindfold exhibitions, taking on some forty competent opponents simultaneously, and defeating a high proportion. They have held records for that sort of achievement, but it may be significant that neither has ever come close to winning the championship of the world over the board, one against one.

Some of the great card players have similar recall. A practical joke often tried on an expert consists in stacking the deck and dealing a hand he has met before. Almost always his recognition of it is instantaneous, and he can replay it, calling attention to the mistakes if any.

An accountant with whom I occasionally play Gin can, after a stand-off, name all the discards in order, and tell whether each was left in the pile or picked.

A brain must contain a rare, recondite, built-in gimmick — a combination photographing, printing and cataloging device — to be capable of such feats. Witnessing them, ordinary people tend to feel discouraged: "How can I hope to compete with somebody like that?" They should feel *en*-couraged, for the feats reveal what can be done. Every normally intelligent human has such powers in some measure. They may be vestigial, but they are susceptible to development and application.

Actually most of us remember much more than we think we do, especially in fields of particular interest to us. A major league pitcher, regarded as a "rock" by his teammates, can list effortlessly the batting peculiarities of any player he has faced during his long career which has taken in at least five leagues. A salesman who barely passed his firm's aptitude tests has made good with a line of more than two hundred products; he remembers the complete price structure, the information in his manual, and the full names and requirements of all of his customers. A young actor is what the profession calls "aquick study"; he can repeat verbatim a long paragraph on hearing it once; he can memorize a part overnight. A diamond dealer can recognize every stone he has ever looped. I mention these four men because each of them has said to me:

"When I sit down to play Gin, I can't remember the cards."

It is true that they *do* not remember the cards, but they *can.*

If you have the same difficulty, you can overcome it, and without making a career of Gin. All you need do is make the effort systematically and consistently. I do not promise that you will suddenly develop the recall of an Edison or a Marshall; I am neither writing an advertisement full of zowie for a memory course, nor compiling such a course. All I propose to do is suggest how you can eradicate your "forgetory" at Gin, or at any other card game for that matter.

There are several common reasons why people forget. Let us examine them one by one. Foremost among them is:

Failure to observe closely in the first place. Take the Lincoln penny, the Jefferson nickel, the Roosevelt dime, on which the heads are all in profile. You handle these coins every day, and have often looked at them. Which way does each head face? Left or right? You are unusual if you can answer correctly about all three.

A college man in whom I am interested recently reported that he had met a girl about whom he was excited.

"What is she like?" I asked.

"Stunning."

"No doubt. Is she a blonde, brunette or redhead?"

"Kind of a dark blonde."

"What's the color of her eyes?"

"Grayish. I'm not sure."

"Is she tall, medium or short?"

"Tall, and she has a fine figure."

I have been presented to the girl. She has hazel eyes. She is rather short, and wears very high heels. She has charm. Perhaps it is unreasonable to expect a young man falling in love to be specific about details. He sees what he wants to see.

Love aside, I think it is good mental training to strengthen the powers of recall by habitually giving them the sound foundation of careful observation of all things of interest, but we are concerned here only with cards.

At Oklahoma Gin, when the first upcard is dealt — at regular Gin when the first discard is made — look at it for one full second, recording in your mind the suit and the rank. If it is a ♠ or ♣, remind yourself that the card is in a black suit. If it is a ♡ or ◊, remind yourself that the card is in a red suit. Look at the corner index again for the rank. You may argue that all of this complicates the memory process, but the reverse is true. Association is an aid to memory, and classification is a kind of association.

Some players use an added method of classification: the ten-count cards in one class, the intermediate cards in another, the lower cards in another. You may want to try it. If it hinders rather than helps you, drop it.

Most people best remember what they see; some best remember what they hear; all remember better when they assimilate something through both eye and ear. So whisper to yourself the suit and rank of each card as it is played.

Short, crisp rhymes are easy to remember. Ask anyone educated in America to quote a famous election slogan, and he is likely to come up with "Tippecanoe and Tyler too" rather than something more recent. I hope you will not consider it childish to try the rhyming method at the Gin table — five jive, four score, and so on. Other rhymes will do as well. You don't have to say them; just think them.

Lack of concentration, which may be due to lack of interest. One night when I was a participant in a team game at Oklahoma Gin. a player suddenly asked, "What was the bid?" He had forgotten the upcard. Noting where his mind was, I suggested a switch to Bridge — not that I preferred it just then. The irony was lost on him, and he was all for Bridge. The other players would have none of it, so he fouled up the Gin game.

The man who is not really interested in Gin — who plays it only to accomodate friends — should stay out of team games. And he should keep the stakes low, lest he lose his shirt. Incidentally, I am opposed to putting anybody in the position where he is compelled, for social or other reasons.

to play a game for which he has no liking.

A man beset by serious problems may sit down to play Gin with the idea that it will help him forget them. He, too, should keep the stakes low. Even though the game may keep his problems out of his consciousness, they will harrass him from the depths. The worried player cannot give the game the concentration it demands; he forgets and blunders.

It is better to try to solve extraneous problems before sitting down at the Gin table. Where no solution can be found, acceptance of the worst eventuality may help. That eventuality may not look so bad as it originally did, and Gin can be a wonderful anodyne.

A strong emotion, notably fear or anger. It is sure to interfere with orderly thinking, including recall. If the source is unrelated to the game, blot out the fear or anger before starting play. If the emotion is the result of some occurrence at the game, pause and reflect. Ask yourself who is doing what, and why he is doing it.

Some card players conduct themselves in a cavalier manner calculated to arouse fear and anger in the opposition. I know one who is adept at Gin and a life master at Bridge. As his total of master points has steadily increased, so has his arrogance.

"You've been acting like a louse," an intimate said. "Why?"

The life master did not deny the allegation. He blandly answered, "To intimidate the dogmeat."

Dogmeat is the unimaginative term used in some Bridge circles to designate any player deemed inferior. It expresses an attitude from which some Gin circles are not free.

Understanding what is behind such an attitude should enable you to cope with it. If you must play with the offender, give him the needle; if you lack the temperament for that, ignore his behavior — study the cards, remember them, give them your best effort. Try to hit him in the bankroll where it will sting.

Needling is part of Gin, just as it is part of Poker. The best antidote is the kind of technique which makes you a winner. When the loser tells you that you have been lucky, yes him, and give him his change.

Crowding. The brain is a spongy substance, literally and figuratively. When an excess of information is poured into it too rapidly, some will spill over. What is an excess at Gin? The average adult can repeat a series of seven or eight digits most of the time; he can, *if he tries,* remember the eight or nine discards in the average Gin hand. Beyond that number, the task may seem to be beyond him, but there are ways of managing it. One good way is to break up the flow of discards into series of three or four — whichever produces the better rhythm in your mind. Look at this array of cards:

♡ ◇ ◇ ♣ ♡ ♠ ♣ ◇ ♣ ♠ ♠ ♡
J 8 2 A 9 Q 2 K 10 2 Q Q

It is a jumble. Now look at the same cards broken into series:

♡ ◇ ◇   ♣ ♡ ♠   ♣ ◇ ♣   ♠ ♠ ♡
J 8 2   A 9 Q   2 K 10   2 Q Q

You can do the same thing in your mind. With practice, you can transpose into more meaningful series, letting the thought take this form: three Queens — the Diamond, Spade and Heart Queens — have been played; three 2's — the Diamond, Club and Spade 2's — have been played. And so on. You need not put the thought into words. Retaining and recalling the images will probably be easier for you, and the images are paramount.

Disuse. You remember automatically the product of eight times eight; you may remember that William of Normandy conquered Harold the Saxon at the Battle of Hastings in 1066. Miss Dinkelspiel of P. S. 97 hammered home the multiplication tables and the dates, but the dates have dropped out of the minds of most of us, whereas we have to do some arithmetic every day. The fact is I remember the Battle of Hastings from a Henty novel, and not because of Miss Dinkelspiel's prodding.

The short-term memory needed to give a Gin hand the best possible treatment can also suffer from disuse. Suppose, at Oklahoma Gin, the upcard is the ♡7, which your opponent refuses. Obviously he does not hold a combination of 7's — he does not hold the ♡9 8 or 6 5. By noting that and playing accordingly, you are making use of the memory of the up-card. You should have no difficulty retaining and recalling that it is in the discard pile.

Again it may seem to you that you are complicating the memory process — that your analysis of your opponent's refusal of the ♡7 is burdening your mind. On the contrary, the analysis is sharpening your memory. Practice will demonstrate that this is true, while improving your technique.

Blocks. A Gin enthusiast in this community was married May 5. His wife complains that he no longer remembers their anniversary. At the card table, he frequently makes errors involving the 5's. Draw your own conclusion.

Repeatedly forgetting some rank or suit may be due to a block. Dredging the cause from the recesses of the memory may result in lifting the block. It may be a task for a psychoanalyst.

The job is done, so the mind dismisses what is no longer useful — the last Gin hand — and turns to other things. That completion is followed by forgetting is all for the best; otherwise our minds would be cluttered with the debris of old hands.

If you have just won the hand, the forgetting is happy. If you have lost it through some error, remember the principle involved, and let the details fade away. Turn your powers of recall to the next hand; try to bring it to happy completion. You have such powers, and exercising them will strengthen them.

All of us remember in fields of endeavor where we perform successfully. There is a reciprocating action at Gin: improving the memory improves play, and improving play improves the memory.

CHAPTER 15

What's Most Necessary?

It is a warm spring evening with traces of pink lingering in the western sky. The earlybirds are at the club, waiting for someone with authority to arrive and set up the Gin games. For a change of pace Latch and Cowboy are playing backgammon. Nearby Proteus and Wander are discussing politics. Clipper occupies a vantage point from which he can observe the game and listen to the discussion. He sequesters some of Proteus's phrases in a corner of his mind for future reference.

As the political discussion subsides Potzer walks in. He tosses a question to the group: "What would you say is the most necessary thing to be a winner at Gin?"

Cowboy grins as he shakes the dice and shoots back an answer: "Holding good tickets."

Clipper snorts. "Over the long haul the cards even up."

"Not exactly," Proteus says. "The cards even up *approximately*—there can be a differential of a couple of percentage points either way for any individual. If you happen to be a poor holder, you've got to play at least that much better than your opponents to break even."

Potzer sighs. "Lately I've been a very good holder but unlucky just the same. Take a hand I held last night. I'll show you." He starts toward a cabinet to fetch a deck of cards.

"Why don't you just describe the hand?" Wander asks. "We can all visualize it."

"I'll remember it better and you can visualize it better when I lay out the cards." Potzer returns with a deck, extracts eleven cards and lays out these ten:

♠	♡	♢	♠	♡	♣	♡	♣	♣	♢
Q	Q	Q	J	J	J	5	4	3	2

"A honey of a hand," Wander says.

"I drew the ♡9 from the stock." Potzer lays it down. "I threw it, and the honey turned to sawdust. Jiffy pounced on it—it gave him a meld of 9's—he knocked with four."

Proteus shakes his head. "You made a mistake throwing the 9."

Clipper nods agreement with Proteus. "I woulda ditched the 5."

Potzer is incredulous. "You mean I should have held the higher card and thrown the lower one?"

"In this situation, yes," Proteus says.

Clipper explains why: "If the 5 woulda given your opponent a meld, it would probably have discombobulated his knock cache."

Potzer ponders, lets the analysis penetrate, scratches his chin. "You're right. I'll have to remember the point."

"It's a sharp one," Cowboy says. He thinks: If the identical situation should arise ten minutes from now, Potzer won't recognize it."

"Getting back to Potzer's question," Wander says, "it's very important to get on the score early."

"One and one equal two," Cowboy says with a leer.

Wander turns his chair and glares at Cowboy. "How's that?"

"No harm meant." Cowboy smiles placatingly.

Latch cuts in quickly. "If you ask me, the most vital thing at Gin is to be able to read your opponent. The arithmetic is simple enough and most hands are finished after a few picks—there isn't too much to remember. You've got to figure out how your opponent's mind is working."

Jiffy saunters in and Cowboy goes, "Ack-ack-ack-ack." Proteus and the others greet him as speedboy. Jiffy says,

"You've evidently been having an interesting gabfest. What's the topic?" Potzer tells him. Jiffy spouts an opinion: "The most necessary thing is remembering what's been discarded and what's been picked from the discard pile by the other fella."

"Also doping out the whys and wherefores," Wander says.

"Especially you've got to remember the knock card," Potzer says.

"Everybody who plays this game regularly remembers those things well enough most of the time," Clipper says. "You've got to really want to win." He recalls a word he saw on the sporting page of his newspaper. "You've got to have desire."

"Who *wants* to lose?" Jiffy asks.

"The neurotic gamblers," Proteus says. "Of course, they do not consciously want to lose, but they are beset by feelings of guilt or mental conflicts which impel them to err again and again."

Cowboy steals a glance at Potzer, then turns toward Proteus. "How do you tell a neurotic from an outright palooka?"

Before Proteus can answer, Jiffy says, "The palooka may be a palooka because he was born a palooka, or because he is a neurotic."

"I guess it takes a head shrinker to make the distinction," Cowboy says.

Jiffy smirks. "Now take our good friend Potzer—"

"Never mind!" Potzer cuts in. "Did you ever check on the amounts you lose by playing so fast? What do you suppose makes you do that?"

Jiffy begins defending himself. "Whatever anyone says about me, I don't slow things down like Sludge."

Clipper makes peace. "Gentlemen, let's omit personalities."

Wander gets back to the original subject. "You've got to have poise. You mustn't let a bad run get you down."

"It helps to get mad at the other guy," Cowboy says.

Proteus laughs. "It helps more to let your opponent get angry while you keep your calm."

"Don't you believe in generating fighting spirit?" Potzer asks.

"Fighting spirit and anger are not synonymous," Proteus answers. "The angry man too often loses control of the game."

"You've got to be tough in the clutch," Wander says.

"It's better to be tough all of the time," Clipper says.

"Forget the hunches and play the probabilities," Jiffy says.

Wander cannot resist the urge to apply the needle. "At your rate of speed, how can you generate hunches *or* calculate the probabilities?"

"The way your mind roams all over the piazza, neither can you," Jiffy retorts.

"Aaa, stop arguing like kids," Clipper says. "You've got to consider the psychological nuances."

Potzer cocks an eyebrow. "Such as?"

"All of them," Clipper says.

"You've got to be able to make a big play from time to time," Cowboy says.

"Gentlemen, you have brought up relevant factors." Proteus pauses, then continues in the manner in which he addresses juries. "But if I had to pick a partner for a partnership game, do you know whom I would choose? Not the trickster, not the man who brings off an occasional brilliancy, not the man whose mind is full of other things. The partner I would want is the man who concentrates on the game all of the time, who knows what is going on, who continually plays the percentages. He not only knows how his opponent's mind works, but how to make it work to the advantage of my team. Yes, I'll take him in preference to the self-styled genius who occasionally piles up a big score but throws away twice as many points because of faulty judgment. Give me the sound, steady player every time."

CHAPTER 16

Invitation from Birdie

High in Van Duyck Towers in mid Manhattan, Birdie and her husband rent an apartment which they use when they want a respite from Vista. The large living room is furnished with prized antiques which she is continually selling and replacing, so what appears to be a luxury more than pays for itself. Tonight she will have the apartment to herself, for her husband is attending a medical conference in Boston. It is spring, and she is in a mood for adventure.

The day has been exciting and fruitful. Birdie spent the morning at the auction of the contents of an old town house which must make way for a skyscraper. She bought a fine Sheraton table and sideboard for a customer who will willingly pay her three times her investment. She took luncheon with the auctioneer, who would have liked to spend the evening with her as well. In the afternoon, at her favorite couturier's she bought a suit and all the accessories. Then she had her hair done.

Her plan for the evening includes dinner with Latch. She wears her new costume. The suit is black silk-shantung, mantailored but moulded to her figure. A diamond clip sparkles from the lapel. A confection of white tulle is draped on top of her cluster of shiny curls.

Latch is proud to be seen with Birdie. He taxis her to an ancient and expensive hofbrau which is patronized by members of his trade association —

"That's some dish with Latch. She's probably an important buyer."

"She's no chicken."

"Maybe not, but she certainly is stacked."

They start with daiquiris. Birdie wants chopped liver, lentil soup, sauerbraten with dumplings, shtrudel and coffee. Latch suggests a bottle of Traminer.

"It's grand goin' out with a man who knows his wines," she trills.

They eat, drink, and discuss the business which is the reason for their being together: the Vista Improvement Association is pushing a redevelopment program right through Birdie's antique shop, and he is chairman of the relocation committee. She contrives a helpless mien as she asks, "Yo goin' to drive po li'l me out of business?"

"Don't worry." Latch pats her hand. "The government will pony up funds, and I guarantee personally that you won't get hurt. You'll wind up with a bigger, better shop which won't cost you a dime."

"Yo a real friend." She gives his hand a squeeze, lets go, demolishes a dumpling. The conversation turns to their favorite game. She says, "Ah sho would enjoy a battle of wits tonight."

"I'd gladly accomodate you myself, but I've got to catch a train home." Latch wishes he didn't have to catch it. "I'm entertainning some of the men. The women will probably organize a Canasta game. You play Canasta, don't you?"

"Yo sweet to make the suggestion. Unfortunately, ah got to stay ovuh in N'yawk." She finishes her shtrudel.

"I know a nice club where you can get a good Gin game." He looks at his timetable and watch. "I could introduce you."

"Ah'd just love that. Too bad yo cain't stay."

The club occupies a suite in a hotel where musty odors blend with that of fresh paint. In a far corner of the main room, four women are playing a version called Persian Rummy. The male habituees have not yet begun to arrive. Jonas, the manager, greets Latch effusively, and bows ceremoniously when he is presented to Birdie.

Clipper saunters over, is presented to her, and for a moment he feels an urge to violate his rule against playing cards with women. His hustler's instinct tells him Birdie will be no mark, and that vitiates the urge.

Jonas gets Latch aside, and sidemouths, "How should I match her up? Maybe Potzer will be around, or ..."

"Go easy on Potzer," Latch says. "Birdie plays a first class game."

Cowboy follows a long corona into the club, stares at Birdie, is tempted to emit a split whistle, emits a cloud of smoke instead. She turns to crush out a cigaret, and to give him a side view of her figure. Jonas presents him to her. Curling a timid smile, she says, "Yo look like a real expert to me."

"Oh, I play at the game." At the moment he feels he can conquer the entire world.

Latch says, "You two will have a nice game. I'm sorry I've got to run."

Birdie again squeezes Latch's hand. Cowboy feels envious. Jonas seats Birdie and Cowboy at the newest table. Jones, himself, brings the cards and score pad. "Set the stakes to suit yourselves. The usual game here is for two or three cents a point."

"A girl has to pay for her experience," Birdie says archly.

Cowboy is magnanimous. "We could make it a cent a point, or even less."

"Cent a point sounds about right," Birdie says. "Oklahoma Gin?"

"Oklahoma suits me." Cowboy breaks open the box and takes out the cards. "Hollywood?"

"Ah just adore Hollywood scorin'," Birdie says. "It's a mite complicated, so would you mind doin' the bookkeepin'?"

"I'll be delighted." Cowboy starts shuffling.

Birdie removes her jacket. "It's kind of wome in here."

[er blouse is sheer white lace, and off-the-shoulder.

The women digress from the complications of Persian
ummy to appraise it.

"She must have *some* sugar daddy."

"You'd think Cowboy would see through her."

"That blouse ought to make it easy. I wish somebody
vould make me a gift of one just like it."

The attendant takes Birdie's jacket, hesitates. "If you'll
excuse me, we can't be responsible for jewelry."

"Ah trust yo-all." Birdie's tone is ingenuous.

Jonas comes over. "It's a fine, beautiful clip. With your
permission, I'll remove it for safe keeping."

"If you think that necessary." Birdie is unworried; the
clip is insured.

They cut. Cowboy deals. The upcard is the ♠Q. After two
picks, Birdie announces, "Ah'm goin' down with nine. Maybe
yo can undercut me, but all the authorities recommend tryin'
to get on score early."

"Very wise." Cowboy's net deadwood count is fifty-one.

"Let's see, it's 'spades double,' Birdie says. "Ah do believe
ah've blitzed yo." She leans over to see that he enters the
score accurately.

Cowboy enters it, looks up into the blouse, looks into
Birdie's eyes. "It couldn't happen to a more charming lady."

Birdie averts her eyes. "Yo do say the most flatterin'
thangs."

In the second game, Cowboy gets on score ahead of her
Encouraged by the success, he begins to speculate — with
the usual result, so that Birdie gets on. He plays a hand
recklessly, holding combinations of picture cards too long,
and she catches him with a mess of them. "Yo bold style of
play has me guessin'," she says. "With a smidgeon of luck,
yo would be ridin' high."

Cowboy softens his voice. "I'd take a chance anywhere
with you."

Birdie smiles mysteriously, and deals. She wins the second game — and the third, which is another shut-out. They start another Hollywood. She is intent upon the cards, while Cowboy is intent upon her. Theirs is the most kibitzed table in the club tonight, and Birdie has cheerful smiles for all the kibitzers. The women from the Persian Rummy group make frequent trips to the rest room so that, in passing, they can see her close up. She has smiles for them, too — with the corners of her mouth.

Curiosity eventually draws Clipper to their table. He tarries long enough to satisfy himself that his estimate of Birdie was correct; then he goes to the desk. "That dame is a solid pro."

"At what?" Jonas asks.

"At Gin. I don't know what else," Clipper says.

"Is Cowboy getting in deep?" Jonas asks.

Clipper gives a short laugh. "That's the big question."

By midnight Birdie is more than seven thousand points ahead of Cowboy. He says, "I'm not doing too well. Just the same, it's a pleasure to play Gin with you."

"Yo certainly a good spote about it." Birdie stares earnestly into his eyes. "No man can buck the kind of run yo been havin'. Ah feel guilty winnin' those gobs of points, and ah'm willin' to give yo a chance to come even. Would yo like to double the stakes?"

Cowboy shrugs. "If you really want to . . ."

Birdie puts an errant curl back in place. "Ah'll be content either way. It's up to yo."

How can Cowboy decline the challenge?" All right, two cents a point it is, the rest of the way."

At the doubled stakes, Cowboy doubles his loss by one o'clock. It is closing time, but they manage to crowd in one more hand — Cowboy wins it by six points. Jonas comes over, inspects the score, puts a consoling hand on Cowboy's shoulder, and says, "You're not going to make that up tonight."

Birdie gives a cluck. "Ah do believe his luck was beginnin to turn."

Cowboy counts out into Birdie's hand the money due her. Despite his protests, she insists on paying both their card fees. She puts on her jacket and reclaims her clip. They walk out together.

As soon as they are alone on the street, Cowboy suggests a snack. "I hate to leave you. Where are you stopping?"

"Ah have an apartment in town," Birdie says, "and ah cain't think of any reason why yo should leave me just yet. Yo can come up with me."

Ebulliently he hails a taxi. In the taxi he starts to put an arm about her — she squirms away. "Careful. Yo puttin' wrinkles in mah new jacket." He decides to be patient. Traffic is light at this hour — they are soon at Van Duyck Towers.

The elevator is fast, and her apartment is close to it. She clicks open the door, and in the dark entrance hall he takes her hand. She pulls it away to switch on lights, shows him into the living room. An Empire sofa with a gold-leafed frame and green satin upholstery catches his eye. He says, "That's elegant. It looks like a museum piece."

"Ah'm glad yo approve o' mah taste," she says. "Antiques are mah passion."

"I hope they're not your only passion," he says.

She points to the sofa. "Yo can buy it if yo've a mind to. While yo think it ovuh, ah'll fix us some coffee."

Although Cowboy would rather by-pass the coffee, he defers to her hospitality. While she bustles about in the kitchen, he looks out the window at the dark masses of brick and stone, and down to the East River on which lights shimmer. Birdie pokes her head in. "Yo wait while ah freshen up." She goes into the bedroom. He wonders whether the river can be seen from it. He thinks, I'll find out soon. She keeps him waiting, waiting. Time is heavy, and he tugs at it. He adjusts his tie, runs a pocket comb through his hair. He walks in the direction she took — "You all right, Birdie?"

"Ah couldn't be feelin' bettuh."

So that door is the one! He turns the knob. The lock holds fast. She chirps, "Wrong door."

Cowboy's self assurance ebbs. He retreats to the living room, sits in the sofa. He hears her leave the bedroom and bustle in the kitchen again. When she returns to the living room, she is wearing black velvet slacks, the tapered kind called capris, and a shell pink angora cardigan with the top button left undone. She is carrying a tray. He jumps up, takes it from her, puts it down on the gold-finished French coffee table. On the tray are a pot of coffee, cups and saucers, a cheese platter, napkins. Also on it are a deck of cards, a score pad, a pencil. She says, "We can play some hot Gin while we're havin' our snack."

"Gin?" Cowboy shakes his head. "I couldn't keep my mind on it."

"Yo don't have to. Ah just wanted to give yo a chance to win back yo money." She leans over, pours the coffee. "Do sit down."

"We'll have lots more chances to play Gin." He tries to pull her close, jolts the table, rattles the cups. A few drops spill over. She jumps away, grabs a napkin, blots up the drops. He says, "I didn't mean to be clumsy."

"Yo not clumsy," she says. "Just a mite impetuous. No hahm done."

Cowboy has waited long enough. He tucks an arm inside hers. "I'd love to see your bedroom." He tries to propel her toward it.

Birdie does not budge. "Nothin' much to see there. Some ordinary pieces."

"That's not what I meant." He squeezes her arm. She disengages the arm. "Mistuh Cowboy, yo have been a perfect gentleman all evenin'. Please don't spoil it now."

He essays logic. "How would going to bed together spoil anything?"

"Well, now, fo one thing, ah'm a happily married woman,"

she says. "Fo another, while ah like yo very much, ah don't like yo that way. Ah'm sho there's plenty other women who do. The one who gets yo will be lucky."

"Uhuh." His mouth feels parched. "Why did you give me the big come-on?"

"Come-on?" She opens her eyes wide, bulges them, raises her eyebrows. "Ah'm afraid yo misinterpreted mah friendliness. Ah thought all yo wanted was to play cyards. Ah never dreamed yo'd turn out to be a wolf."

There are men who would persist in such a situation. Cowboy is not one of them; he stands meekly like an ox in a pen.

Birdie subdues a yawn. "Don't act like the world is comin' to an end. Ah'm sorry ah disappointed yo. Take some coffee."

Cowboy regains a little of his composure. "I'd better take my leave."

As soon as he has gone, Birdie inspects the coffee table, satisfies herself it is unstained. Carrying the tray back to the kitchen, she deplores the waste of good coffee. She dutifully telephones her husband, and assures him of her eternal love. "Ah miss yo dreadfully, sugar."

The capris and the cardigan go carefully on hangers. She gets into a filmy nightgown, and snuggles under the bedsheet. Being in bed alone pleases her. The doctor has been randy of late, but tonight she will not be bothered.

Glossary

ADVERTISE — Also bait, fish, send out a salesman. To discard tactically, trying to lure a wanted card from an opponent.

BAIT — See Advertise. Also a card used to advertise; see salesman.

BLITZ — Also schneid, schneider, shut-out, skunk. To win a game in which the loser has scored no points. Also such a game.

BLOCK — To hold on to a card which the other player needs.

BOX — One deal played to completion. Also the winner's score after such a deal.

BOX BONUS — The added score for winning a box, usually twenty-five points.

CATCH — To get a particular card or hand.

CAPTAIN — Where two are partners against one, the partnership member who handles the cards and makes final decisions for the partnership.

COMBINATION — Two cards of the same rank or consecutive in the same suit.

COUNT — The total points assigned to each card according to rank; the point total of the deadwood in a hand.

CUT — After the shuffle, to separate the deck into packets and change their order.

CUTTHROAT — One of the descriptive names given to three-handed Gin, where a three-column score is kept and each player is on his own.

DEAL — To distribute cards to the players.

DECK — Also pack. All the cards used in the game.

DEAD — Said of cards which are in the discard pile.

DEADWOOD — The unmatched cards in a hand.

DEUCE — Any 2.

DISCARD — After picking, to reduce the hand to ten cards by placing one face up on top of the discard pile.

DISCARD PILE — The pile on which each player in turn places his discards.

DRAW — Also pick. See pick.

FACE CARD — Also picture card. Any K, Q or J.

FISH — Also advertise, bait, send out a salesman. See advertise; see bait.

FLASH — To expose a card.

GAME — Completion of the number of deals which enable either of the players to reach the required total, usually one hundred points.

GAME BONUS — The additional score for winning a game, usually one hundred points.

GIN — A hand consisting entirely of matched cards.

GO DOWN — After a player has knocked or gone Gin, to place the hand face up on the table.

GO GIN — To complete and announce a Gin hand; see Gin.

GROUP — Three or four cards of the same rank in a hand.

GUT CARD — A card which completes a broken sequence. For example, you hold the ♠8 6; the ♠7 is the gut card.

HAND — The cards dealt to a player; the cards he holds at any stage.

HOLLYWOOD — The method of scoring where three games between two players are concurrently in progress. Hollywood scoring may be extended to more games by agreement of the players.

INCORRECT HAND — Any hand which, after discarding, contains more or less than ten cards.

INCORRECT KNOCK — Any knock when the deadwood in the knocker's hand is in excess of the maximum knocking count.

JOKERS — Extra cards not used in most Rummy games; Persian Rummy is an exception.

KIBITZ — To observe the action without participating; the accent is on the first syllable.

KIBITZER — One who kibitzes; the accent remains on the first syllable.

KNAVE — Any Jack.

KNOCK — To announce that play of the hand is terminated, immediately before going down.

KNOCKING COUNT — Also knocking point. The maximum deadwood count with which a player may knock.

LAY — Also matched cards, meld, run, set, spread. See set.

LAY OFF — After a knock, to match cards from the non-knocker's hand against any of the knocker's sets. There is no laying off when a player has gone Gin.

MATCHED CARDS — Also meld, run, set, spread. See set.

MECHANIC — A cheat, especially one who plies his trade by sleight-of-hand, or by using a stacked deck.

MELD — To lay down a set after a knock or when a player has gone Gin. Also a lay, matched cards, run or set. See set.

OKLAHOMA GIN — The variation in which the upcard determines the knocking count: see upcard. Do not confuse with just Oklahoma, a different form of Rummy.

ORIGINAL HAND — The first ten cards dealt to a player.

PICK — Also draw. In a playing turn, to take the top card from the stock or the discard pile; any card so taken.

PICTURE CARD — Also face card. See face card.

REDEAL — Another deal by the same player after one which was nullified; to perform the task of redealing.

READERS — Marked cards.

REFUSE — To decline the right to pick the upcard or an opponent's discard.

REDUCER — Any low card picked or held to reduce the deadwood count in a hand.

RIFFLE — To shuffle the deck by separating it into two approximately equal packets, and intermingle the cards at random with a movement of the fingers.

SALESMAN — A card discarded to advertise. See advertise.

SCHNEID, SCHNEIDER — Also blitz, shut-out, skunk. See blitz.

SEND OUT A SALESMAN — Also advertise, bait, fish. See salesman; see advertise.

SEQUENCE — Three or more consecutive cards in the same suit.

SET — Also lay, matched cards, meld, run, spread. Three or more cards of the same rank, or consecutive in the same suit; a group or sequence.

SHADERS — Cards marked by shading the backs.

SHILL — A cheat's confederate.

SHINER — A reflecting device used by a cheat.

SHUFFLE — Also wash; to randomize the cards before cutting. and dealing.

SHUT-OUT — Also blitz, schneid, schneider, skunk. See blitz.

SKUNK — Also blitz, schneid, schneider, shut-out. See blitz.

SPECULATE — to pick an opponent's discard which produces a combination, not a complete set.

SPREAD — Also lay, meld, run, set. See set.

STACK THE DECK — To arrange the cards in known places in it.

STAND-OFF — A deal played to a tie.

STOCK — The undealt part of the deck from which the players may pick in turn.

STRANGERS — Unrelated cards in a hand.

TREY — Any 3.

UNDERCUT — After a knock, to expose a hand with a deadwood count equal to or lower than the knocker's; to reduce to such a count by laying off.

UNDERCUT BONUS — A predetermined number of points awarded to the undercutter in addition to the net difference in their deadwood counts.

UNDERCUT PENALTY — The undercut bonus from the loser's point of view.